DATE DUE

DEMCO 38-296

Why I Can't Read Wallace Stegner

and Other Essays

Why I Can't Read Wallace Stegner

and Other Essays

A Tribal Voice

ELIZABETH COOK-LYNN

The University of Wisconsin Press

The University of Wisconsin Press
114 North Murray Street
Madison, Winconsin 53715

3 Henrietta Street
London WC2E 8LU, England

5 4 3 2 1

Printed in the United States of America

Library of Congress Cataloging-in-Publication Data
Cook-Lynn, Elizabeth.
    Why I can't read Wallace Stegner and other essays: a tribal voice /
  Elizabeth Cook-Lynn.
      172 p.   cm.
      Includes bibliographical references and index.
      ISBN 0-299-15140-9 (cloth: alk. paper).
      ISBN 0-299-15144-1 (pbk.: alk. paper)
      1. American literature—Indian authors—History and criticism—Theory, etc.
  2. Stegner, Wallace Earle, 1909–   —Criticism and interpretation.   3. Indians of
  North America—Intellectual life.   4. Indians in literature.   I. Title.
  PS153.I52C576   1997
  810.9'897—dc20   96-18557

To the indigenous writer in the modern world

Contents

Preface

To talk about my career as a college professor, I must speak of affirmative action, the federal policy that arose from the notion that unusual action had to be taken if there was ever to be equality in higher education and the workplace. At the close of the ninth decade of this remarkable century, my admission is notable only because so many who have benefited from affirmative action are so reluctant to admit their participation in and gratitude for a national effort to combat institutional, systemic racism. They've given in to the emotion of Richard Rodriguez's autobiography, *Hunger of Memory* (1982). Saul D. Alinsky, author of *A Pragmatic Primer for Realistic Radicals* (1971), has disappeared from the streets, and a black man who declares that affirmative action has damaged him sits on the Supreme Court bench.

For me it was never just a matter of getting a job and becoming a part of the mainstream; instead, it was that the entire history of America, vis-à-vis the continent's indigenous population, had to be rewritten, and the place to do it was in the nation's colleges and universities. New narratives were required, I said. Tribal (First Nation) interests had to be maintained. Small wonder that I became disillusioned. At the close of two decades, I'd had enough and left my tenured faculty position for the open hills and prairies of home. What I see now is a backlash so severe it makes me shudder. The courts have been stacked, Oliver North runs for a seat in the U. S. Senate, and racist science in the name of the bell curve flourishes.

For many of us, the 1960s were doubtful times. During that tumultuous decade I had undergone severe revision. I had moved back to my homelands in South Dakota to take a job teaching English at the largest high school in the state—a failed marriage, four children, and a dog and cat in my company. One of my ex-husband's relatives from Cheyenne River Sioux Indian Reservation, a community worker in the city schools, welcomed me home by saying, "They hired you here because they didn't really know who you were. They thought you were Elizabeth Cook from Carlsbad, New Mexico, not Elizabeth Renville/Bowed Head/Irving/Tatiopa from Crow Creek and Sisseton of the Sioux Nation." The implication in his ambivalent welcome was that Indians were not hired in these state-supported schools in South Dakota, where people had not yet heard very often of affirmative action, and my example was mere fluke. Having been born and raised on an Indian reservation in a place which has one of the largest Indian populations, highest Indian unemployment, and the lowest wage and poverty line in the country, I had no reason to refute his unsolicited observation.

After a year of teaching in an overcrowded high school beset with un-resolved issues of racism and drug abuse, I was approached by a college professor who has since left the Education Department at University of South Dakota (to raise swine in Arkansas, the rumor is). We went to lunch with Jim Emery, Sr., an old friend of my parents, and the two of them (out beating the bushes for Indians who held undergraduate de-grees and were enrolled citizens of the Sioux Nation) politely suggested that I should enroll in a master's degree program designed especially for Indians at USD. This government-funded effort to "act affirmatively" in qualifying American Indians to work in educational institutions in the state was, as far as I knew, one of the first of its kind and the beginning of my rather curious academic career.

There are no small ironies in the results of this inauspicious begin-ning. Though the master's degree in this program for Indians was in Counseling and Psychology (based on the idea there was something unhealthy in the dropout rate of native students from area schools), I took the degree and went on to do research and writing in the inchoate field of Native American Indian Studies. My work has turned out to be unabashedly based on the idea that there is probably nothing unhealthy in Indians dropping out of racist and damaging school systems to which they are routinely subjected. It appears instead that there is something systemically unhealthy in the schools, themselves, in their false history based on the assumptions of a European body of thought which suggests that the American Indian experience is somehow a lesser one.

The second and, perhaps, more predictable irony is that my teaching and writing was not destined to be done in the state of South Dakota. There were no offers for counseling positions in the state, nor for teach-ing posts, but an offer of a tenured faculty position came from Eastern Washington University, an unassuming regional university surrounded by the several powerful Indian tribes of Washington and Idaho, which, in the throes of change, wanted to develop "affirmative" strategies for meeting the educational needs of the native populations on their own terms. In the process of that development, they wanted to hire native faculty members.

It was a conversion experience for everyone concerned. Only much later, following the backlash to affirmative action articulated success-fully in such litigation as the Bakke Case, the subsequent writings of several "minority" scholars such as Shelby Steele and Richard Rod-griquez, and the flawed thinking which emerged during the Reagan presidency, was affirmative action dismissed as a noble idea. For my part, the affirmative action years gave me a brief vision of grace, the hope of a transcendent time when people like myself would be welcomed as *American Indians* into America's modern debates concerning society and knowledge which raged then and continue to rage today. I wrote and published poetry, fiction, and scholarly papers, did further graduate studies at the University of Nebraska in Lincoln, and in 1985 (along with my illustrious colleagues Dr. Beatrice Medicine, Dr. William Willard, and Professor Roger Buffalohead), founded a journal of Native Studies called the *Wicazo Sa Review*, which would eventually be read by scholars across the country in such diverse places as the Harvard Law School, the Oglala Lakota Community College, the New York Public Library, Mexico, Canada, and fourteen other foreign countries.

I left my tenured faculty position in 1990, only when it became clear that there was no longer the institutional support and interest I needed to do my work. As affirmative action was no longer at home in the academy, neither was I, though I admire those American Indian scholars who have the courage to continue. Today, I do not teach on a regular basis, nor am I associated with any university, but I will be forever grateful to my colleagues at EWU who, in their emeritus description of me said this: "Elizabeth Cook-Lynn came to Eastern in 1971 to teach in the English Department and the emerging Indian Education Program. She was one of Indian Studies' secondary founders and also, in many ways, its conscience."

Introduction

This volume in five sections is designed to raise and discuss issues that are some of the most central and crucial questions in the field of American Indian Studies. The first section suggests that the book and media culture of America has had an enormous impact on its citizens, both native and nonnative. Now that this culture is being examined and criticized by those persons whose intellectual backgrounds are deeply embedded in the oral traditions of the native tribes of America, new visions are in the offing, mistaken ideas about the native past can be reexamined, and concerns that have not been a part of the broad public dialogue can now be addressed.

Part 1 discusses the emergence of the native voice in critical scholarship. My reviews of the books *Wounded Knee, 1973,* by Stanley David Lyman (University of Nebraska Press, 1991), *The Broken Cord,* by Michael Dorris (Harper and Row, 1989), *Black Eagle Child,* by Ray A. Young Bear (University of Iowa Press, 1992), and *Black Hills, White Justice,* by Edward Lazarus (HarperCollins, 1995), are presented as pieces which typify the scholarly renderings of diverse publications in Indian topics of the last decade. I attempt here to create a dialogue concerning the principles of critical analysis, which I believe should be the work of Native American Studies scholars. I maintain that when the ethical relationship between tribal nationhood and the imagination is ignored or falsified, flawed scholarship is the result.

Two essays, "Why I Can't Read Wallace Stegner" and "A Centennial Minute from Indian Country," appear in part 2, entitled "Dispossession." These pieces outline patterns of injustice that stem not only from the tribal imagination silenced or overwhelmed by Western writers for whom Stegner is an icon but, more significantly, perhaps, from the oppressive Christian religion of colonizers who came into Sioux country to change the world.

Part 3 asks the question, "Who Will Tell the Stories?" How the native people of my Indian nation (the Sioux) joined the lit-crit wars is the subject of the essay, "The Relationship of a Writer to the Past." The novel *Hanta Yo* (1979), one of the most incendiary pieces of fiction of the time, written by a white woman from Washington State who claimed the book was "the Indian *Roots*," is used to illustrate the point that tribal models of literary criticism emerged as major vehicles of tribal intellectual empowerment. The second essay in this section, "The American Indian Fiction Writers," condemns what critics have called *cosmopolitanism* in contemporary fiction and argues for decolonization through third-world *nationalism*.

"Women's Lives" is the title of part 4. Two essays, "The American Indian Woman in the Ivory Tower" and "The Big Pipe Case," focus upon some of the moral questions Indian women face in today's society. They illustrate the parameters that Indian women experience both as potential professionals and as mothers of their nations.

The last part, entitled "The Last Word," adds some personal notes to the questions I raise. Before I am anything, I am a Dakota Winyan, woman of the Dakotapi. Finally, I comment briefly on what I see as America's racism, the disastrous dismissal of indigenous mythology, and the failure of metaphor in the modern world. In the process, I challenge readers to understand how important it is for indigenous peoples to honor the past as they participate in the future.

Part One

THOUGHTS ON THE ART
OF REVIEWING BOOKS

Part One

Thoughts on the Art of Reviewing Books

A good way to begin an academic career is to write critical pieces on what is called art and scholarship, because they force the writer to be analytic and thoughtful. They require, too, that scholars acquire some knowledge about and confidence in their own taste in such works.

While writing reviews of books is thought by many to be a nasty thing to do, a mean activity engaged in by the truly perverse, its importance to American Indian communities cannot be overestimated, since mainstream sensibilities and cultures are often patronizing and oppressive, which results in damaging misinformation.

This statement is made neither out of anger nor apology, as it might have been when I first started writing what is called literary criticism. It is, rather, suggestive of the need to create a healthy discussion of point of view, one of the essential elements of fiction as well as scholarship. Besides, it can be great fun!

In fact, when I look at my own career as a writer/scholar, I see evidence to support the idea that I began to write and publish because I really wanted to become a literary critic, and it seemed to me, though others disagree, to be somehow unfair, cowardly, and graceless to critique another's work if my own wasn't out there in the full glare. I think I felt it to be analogous to behaving like the Catholic priest who makes the rules about marriage but doesn't play the game.

Thus, when some obscure critic from Arizona wrote of my first attempt at novel writing, *From the River's Edge*, in the *New York Times* book review section, that I had a great idea for a story but didn't know how to write, I felt appropriately mortified and momentarily filled with self-contempt even as I felt liberated, cleansed, blasted. I felt the tyranny of

3

a bold voice rising up against my pitiful arrogance, drawing me into an intellectual and literary cesspool where we are all pariahs.

I remembered John Hollander's review of "Howl" by Allen Ginsberg, written for the *Partison Review* before I had ever published a word, in which he said, "It is only fair to Allen Ginsburg . . . to remark on the utter lack of decorum of any kind in his dreadful little volume. . . . 'Howl' is meant to be a noun, but I can't help taking it as an imperative."

I thought it to be a wonderful showing of the courage and beastliness it takes to say what one means in no uncertain terms. I was disappointed, therefore, when, in a much later essay, he said in a troubled tone, like a shopper suffering from buyer's remorse,

This review was written in my youth and in a sort of worked-up high dudgeon which echoes the high-camp-prophetic mode of "Howl"'s front matter, and which may have masked some of my disappointment in a turn I saw an old friend and poetic mentor to have taken. I only regret now that I hadn't given "America" and "In a Supermarket in California" time to register; I should have certainly commended them. As for not foreseeing that Allen Ginsberg would provide so much hymnody and doctrine to the counterculture which was soon to emerge, I have no regrets, having no stake in prophecy.

There were others that I loved, many reprinted in the Henderson work. For example, in 1961 a critic for the *San Francisco Chronicle* wrote of *Out of My League* by George Plimpton, "At first thought this seems flimsy substance for a real, live, grown-up book. It turns out it is," and there was the *New Yorker*'s assessment in 1981 of Toni Morrison's *Tar Baby*: "Heavy-handed, and ultimately unintelligible. . . . topples into dreadful pits of bombast."

I hope we don't need to look for some kind of wimpy rejoinder or simpering disclaimer now just because Ms. Morrison has been awarded the Nobel Prize for Literature.

The *New Statesman* in a 1974 review of *Fear of Flying*, by Erica Jong, said, "This crappy novel, misusing vulgarity to the point where it becomes purely foolish . . . represents everything that is to be loathed in American Fiction." So far as I know, the *New Statesman* has not backed down, even though the book has become a classic and some twenty or more other languages have managed to translate Jong's English vulgarisms into their own.

Whether or not I agree with the above-mentioned critiques, I am certain that I don't agree with William Stafford, the renowned American poet who, in a flash of despondency and futility, once said,

It has sometimes occurred to me that the literary world would be much improved if critics just wrote the literature in the first place, thus avoiding that roundabout process in which the author struggles inside the complex of his book, like Laocoon contending with myriad problems, while the critic whisks through the finished book in a few minutes and immediately spots the gross blunders the author has taken a year or more to make.

I disagree because the imagination and the intellect must be held accountable to humanity, and I know of no way other than "critical" evaluation by one's fellow human beings to say what the accountability amounts to in terms of our creative lives, intellectual pursuits, and human communities. For those who don't buy that argument, there is, of course, day-time television, the prime-time miniseries, or any John Wayne movie.

The issue of evaluating what is thought to be scholarship, that is, scientific inquiry, research, and other intellectual study is even more essential to the development of the processes of explication in social history and attitudes in American institutional thought. For the past three decades, American Indian scholars have published a considerable body of that kind of academic work.

Two American Indian scholars, Jeannette Henry and Rupert Costo, editors and publishers at The Indian Historian Press, Inc. in San Francisco, began this work by publishing a quarterly in Native Studies, the *Indian Historian*, as well as a series of well-received books in the 1970s and early 80s. Much of this is now, unfortunately, routinely ignored by many of the new scholars who claim to be Native American Studies practitioners. The Henry-Costo canon, much of it supported by the Ford Foundation and other academic organizations, became crucial to the early work done in writing and research. It was discontinued when the editors retired, and many scholars feel that it has left a noticeable empty space. They published not only their own works, but the works of many of the major native scholars: Medicine, Ortiz, Momaday, Deloria, Forbes, McNickle, Bean, Azbill, Stands-in-Timber, Herman, Carter, Seelatsee, Harjo, Sohappy, Sekequaptewa, Fixico, Warren, and Oaks to name only a handful.

The critical work started by natives in the last few decades goes on, of course. The Sioux scholar, Vine Deloria, a professor of American Indian Studies, History, Law, and Religious Studies at the University of Colorado at Boulder, who began his notable academic career with such books as *Custer Died for Your Sins* and *We Talk, You Listen*, has continued to assess works written about Indians in a significant way. In 1992 recently, he published a review in the *American Indian Quarterly* of a book by Dr. James A. Clifton, *The Invented Indian: Cultural Fictions and Government Policies* (1990), a collection of essays by a number of contemporary scholars in the social sciences, and had this to say:

If this collection of essays is placed in the proper political context, that is, in the arena in which the struggle for authority and control of definitions is primary, we can properly evaluate the contents of the book and come to some intelligent conclusions. A review of the respective essays and a demonstration of the errors and hidden agendas may be useful in showing that these are indeed second-rate scholars on a holy mission of stopping the barbarian hordes (Indians) at the gates before they overwhelm the old citadels of comfortable fiction.

This paragraph, while more blunt than suits the taste of many, states clearly the issue of the influence of modern works on Indians and the tacit reasoning behind the resistance to the appropriate development of the vantage points from which many of the dissenting native voices are said to emerge, that is, affirmative action and Native American Studies as an academic discipline.

Indian-owned and edited newspapers such as *Indian Country Today*, formerly known as the *Lakota Times* of Rapid City, South Dakota, have joined in the dialogue in diverse ways: legitimate news, editorial writing, features, and letters to the editors. Here is an example of how the desire to review what is written about Indians is not just an academic endeavor but one that arises in ordinary lives.

11/10/94—*Indian Country Today*
Lakota Woman was a big disappointment / To the Editor: I saw the movie *Lakota Woman*, and I was very disappointed to say the least. Especially the scene at the Custer County Courthouse. I was never standing on the steps with those police. Instead, I was being fire-hosed to the ground by the white police. Every time I stood up, they would hose me down again. Also, they never showed how my boyfriend, Bob High Eagle, was beat up by the police because he was trying to protect me. If people want to make a movie they should show what really happened, instead of falsifying the facts just to make money. I do not appreciate the way I am portrayed in the movie. I hope Mary Crow Dog and Jane Fonda made a lot of money out of portraying me the way they did because they never had my permission to do so. /s/ Sarah Bad Heart Bull.

My point is that there is now a public voice in native critical analysis, and it comes from many sources. The following pages reproduce several of my previously published critical essays that I consider to be ancillary to the work in criticism begun by Costo, Deloria, and Henry. They illustrate, in terms of subject matter and attitude, an effort to continue *the analysis in a tribal voice* of works about Indians being published in this century. The thrust of such an analysis is to give some balance to scholarly debate on a variety of subjects.

1

Wounded Knee, 1973

The following is what I had to say about Stanley David Lyman's Wounded Knee, 1973: A Personal Account, *a book composed of the diaries of a bureaucrat who has, by now, become archetypal. This review was assigned to me in 1993 by a history journal.*

Diaries are meant to bare one's inner thoughts, yet contend thoughtfully and appropriately with history. They are to suggest the relationship of people to time and place; at the same moment, they reveal inner life and give meaning and insight to events. A book with the title *Wounded Knee, 1973* has the special obligation to search for meaning in one of the most profound and important events in contemporary indian history.

The posthumous diaries that make up this volume by Stanley David Lyman, who was then superintendent of the Pine Ridge Agency, begin on February 22, 1973, and end on July 13, 1973, giving the reader the briefest of glimpses into the "takeover" by the American Indian Movement (AIM) led by Russell Means (Oglala), Dennis Banks (Chippewa), Carter Camp (Osage), and the Belcourt brothers (Chippewa) of a tiny hamlet in South Dakota, the site of the killing of over three hundred unarmed Minneconjous in 1890.

Though it is always risky to publish what some would like to consider the important work of a writer after his death because it is no longer possible to have face-to-face consultation, this publication ends up being particularly irrelevant to those who may desire its inclusion in historical collections and even odious to Indian historians who now believe the historic protest at Wounded Knee in 1973–74 to be instrumental as an important beginning of a new age of Indian survival. The Minneconjou Sioux traditionalist, Arvol Looking Horse (who was barely out of his teens in 1973) in a recent *Life* magazine interview called "100 Years of Solitude," says that the "1974 protest was the beginning of the mending of the Sacred Hoop of the Sioux Nation," thus giving voice to the Lakota assessment of that event, which differs considerably from Lyman's position.

The Lyman manuscript does none of the analysis necessary to live up to its title, though its editors have had two decades to examine the event's consequences. It is, instead, a work made up of the fragments of day-to-day note-taking by a white bureaucrat representing the federal presence on Indian lands and is useful only as an examination of the frightening isolation from the Indian world in which these bureaucrats live and work. Such biographies have become a genre in Indian/white historiography, and when examined within that context, it is easy to see that the more things change, the more they stay the same. One is reminded that James McLaughlin, superintendent of the Standing Rock Sioux Reservation Agency at the time of Sitting Bull's assassination during the first Wounded Knee protest of 1890, wrote annual reports and from them compiled his memoirs, intending (among other thing) to defend the federal presence on Indian lands and condemn Sitting Bull's leadership in opposing the Allotment Act. Today, there is wide acknowledgement in Indian Studies research that through this turn-of-the-century legislation, Indians lost two-thirds of their treaty-protected lands, a devastating economic blow to tribalism. McLaughlin's memoirs, published in his reflective old age, serve only to obfuscate the failure in relations of trust, which is the reality of Indian historical experience of that era.

In reassessing the events at Wounded Knee, Lyman, like Mclaughlin, shows little awareness of what is really happening to Indians on Indian lands through the actions of the federal bureaucracy he represents. He does not mention the brutal midcentury federal Indian policy called Termination and Relocation, which was one of the major causes for the protest. There is no attention to the scandal of corrupt tribal/federal trust relationships; little illumination of poverty, land use, water issues, or state/tribal jurisdictional conflicts; and no mention of the flooding of 550 square miles of treaty-protected Indian lands for hydropower on the Missouri River, which displaced thousands of Sioux Indians in the 1950s and 1960s. Nothing is said of the events at Alcatraz, which preceded those at Wounded Knee in 1973, of the torture and murder of Raymond Yellow Thunder by local whites, or of the stabbing of Wesley Bad Heart Bull by a white man, murders that must be seen in the context of a series of separate killings of unarmed Indians at the time. There is nothing of the problems of racism in South Dakota and nothing about the brutality toward Indians in the educational system.

Rather, in his modern assessment of the federal presence on Indian lands, Lyman spends much of his time assigning pejorative labels to the people of the American Indian Movement and defending the beseiged Oglala tribal president at Pine Ridge, Dick Wilson, whose removal was called for in a grassroots referendum. Lyman says the members of AIM are "trained revolutionaries," "lost men," "violently angered," just as McLaughlin called Sitting Bull a "recalcitrant obstructionist to federal purpose" and a "danger to his people." Lyman's diary entries show that while he knows his purpose as superintendent is to defend the federal bureaucracy, he resents being seen as a protector of this failed legacy.

In one of his final entries he describes a "grandstanding" Senator James Abourezk, a South Dakota native born and raised on the Rosebud Reservation, whose law offices in Rapid City, SD, now handle some litigation for the tribes. When the senator criticizes his handling of the petition to abolish tribal government, which was one of the initial events alluded to in an early February diary entry, his bitterness is palpable:

It is very disappointing to see the senator today [June 16, 1973] take what appeared to be a purely political position. I was disappointed and disgusted at the shallowness of the Senator's questions. Tomorrow, where the witnesses will likely be Russell Means and the Bellecourts and the headmen and chiefs of the reservation . . . well, I just hate to think of it. They are going to be very vindictive and hostile toward the Bureau and Abourezk is going to eat it up. So Wyman Babby and Stan Lyman are going to be roasted over a hot fire all day long tomorrow. It's pretty sad that a senator of the United States is willing to approach a situation as explosive as this one by falling into the same old trap of making the Bureau of Indian Affairs a whipping boy, just as it has been down through the years. And, of course, this solves no problems.

At one point in his diaries, he says he is told by the Justice Department that it had accepted a stand in the negotiations that the Tribal Chairman, Dick Wilson, had already refused to accept, and he complains that he is "put in the position of convincing the elected leadership of the Oglala to accept a decision that has already been made." He "disapproves" of being put in this position, an odd and puzzling complaint from a man whose function as superintendent of an Indian agency is to follow federal policy, which has been in conflict with tribal governmental wishes for as long as anyone can remember.

Feeling frustrated and beaten, Lyman asserts in his July 13, 1973, diary entry that Wounded Knee is now "a symbol of hate, frustration, and failure." Nothing could be further from the Indian reality then or now.

To the Oglala on whose land the grave site is located, to the Minneconjou whose ancestors are buried there, and to other Lakota/Dakota peoples who have concern for their relatives, the symbol of Wounded Knee has never been that. It is a holy place where the people go to weep for their lost loved ones and pray for the continuation of the human spirit.

In fairness, it may be that we often know the significance of an event only in retrospect, and these diaries, seemingly taken word-for-word from notes written hurriedly and under strenuous conditions, perhaps do not do justice to the writer's thoughts. Yet, Lyman's inability to bring insight into what the uprising might mean to future generations of Indians and his editor's isolation from current Indian reservation life makes this book, published by the rather prestigious University of Nebraska Press, a disappointing addition to the many works published on this event and a violation of the function of historical diaries.

Lyman's refusal to see that the takeover of 1973, the rise of the American Indian Movement and the reservation activism of the period, and the ongoing traditionalist influence had the potential to change Indian lives, the bureau, tribal government, and federal/tribal relations forever is disturbingly common to analysts of Indian affairs. His final point that: "People are beginning to come back in; the BIA building is once again at the service of Indian business," is sad and dangerous to the future of our lives as Indian people because it does not recognize that the deconstruction of colonial institutions on Indian lands must be the inevitable function of the historic events at Wounded Knee in 1973.

Following the uprising, Lyman was almost immediately transferred to the Phoenix office in Arizona and died six years later. If Ronald Reagan, as president, was "sleepwalking through history," as Haynes Johnson charged in his recent (1991) book of that name, surely Stanley David Lyman and other federal bureaucrats who work for the federal government on Indian lands must be examined by historians as potential and accompanying sleepwalkers.

2

The Broken Cord

My review of the book The Broken Cord *by one of the most successful writers on Indian topics of our time, Michael Dorris, drew a four-page personal letter from the author, utter silence from others, but comments of agreement from many native women. This piece was published in the* Wicazo Sa Review *in 1989 and, though it was not submitted to any other journal, there is some doubt in my mind that it would have been accepted for publication elsewhere, since the book was a best seller reviewed very favorably in many scholarly circles.*

First there was the *broken hoop*, a signal of the end of Sioux nationhood, a metaphorical device in modern scholarly research created by a University of Nebraska professor named John Neihardt in his acclaimed *Black Elk Speaks* (1932). An ethnographic biography, that book has become a classic. Now there is the *broken cord*, a figurative harbinger of the death of the race, created in an autobiographical polemic published by Harper and Row called *The Broken Cord* (1989). There is plenty of reason to think that this book, too, will become a classic, for there seems to be no end to the interest that people have in declaring the Sioux dead or dying.

Written by the acclaimed author, Michael Dorris, former chair of American Indian Studies at Dartmouth College, *The Broken Cord* is the poignant story of the adoption by Dorris of a Sioux boy afflicted with fetal alcohol syndrome and the twenty-year struggle to come to terms with his adopted son's affliction. Dorris, an "expert on Native Americans," according to the jacket blurb, was one of the first unmarried men in the United States "to legally adopt a very young child, an affectionate Sioux Indian he named Adam," whom he found in 1971 through ARENA, a national adoption service that "attempted to match would-be parents with available children." He was assisted in the search by a social worker with the New Hampshire Catholic Charities and the South Dakota State Welfare Office in Pierre, South Dakota.

11

If you want a classical review of the book I refer you to Patricia Guthrie's piece published in a recent *New York Times Book Review*, entitled "Alcohol's Child: A Father Tells His Tale." She says that Mr. Dorris has raised the questions of what to do with pregnant women who insist on drinking and how one can protect unborn children from fetal alcohol syndrome, questions that Guthrie calls "Solomonic" and "haunting," and she suggests that this book should be required reading for those who want or need answers to these questions.

I do not intend here to write a *New York Times* kind of book review. Rather, I intend to write from the heart, the wrenching opinion of a Dakota *unchi*, born and raised on a Sioux Reservation in South Dakota, whose four children and two grandsons are citizens of the Sioux Nation, one whose family members are enrolled at Cheyenne River, Crow Creek, Yankton, Sisseton, and Rosebud, four generations of us, at this moment alive and well, walking the earth and remembering who we are. I mention this because I believe that *The Broken Cord* is a dangerous book for those of us still committed to ideas inherent in the *tiospsye* concept of reciprocity, which the Dakotapi devised as a way to live.

The Broken Cord begins by telling us the story of Adam's early, prenatal abuse and neglect as an infant, which resulted in his affliction with fetal alcohol syndrome (FAS): "When I bathed him I discovered the marks of IV's and catheters, souvenirs of his bouts with pneumonia," says Dorris. "His ankles and wrists were scored with thin white scars . . . evidence of that time when, as an infant, he had been tied into a crib by his abusive, neglectful mother," a Lakota woman who, we are told, died of alcohol poisoning and whom Dorris and his wife, novelist Louise Erdrich, accuse and blame throughout the book. "She had no right to inflict such harm, even from the depth of her own ignorance," says Erdrich, who, in the preface to the text, approves the idea of enforced incarceration of such women because "she had no right to harm her, and our, son."

The argument that it is the blood mothers of these FAS children who must be punished is further articulated when Dorris says, "A choice, no matter how buried its trigger, had been made by one party in this sorrowful transaction and not by the other. My ultimate allegiance was to that person Adam was not allowed to be, to the baby carried by every woman who wouldn't . . . or who couldn't . . . stay alcohol-free for nine crucial months."

Erdrich agrees, and in a few chilling, precise paragraphs says she would eliminate FAS and FAE *"anyway I could."* If you don't agree, she says bitterly, "Go sit beside the alcohol-affected while they learn how to add. Dry their frustrated tears." She gives support in this manner to the frightening statistics promulgated by her husband's study that from one-fourth to one-half of the populations on some Sioux reservations are affected by FAS. Mona Richards, special education counselor at Little Wound, Elaine Beaudreau, vice president of Oglala Lakota Tribal College, and Sharon Cuny, an elementary grade teacher, seem to agree with Dorris's findings. "At least a third of the population of any school system on the reservation, a third of the student body, have some kind of emotional or learning problem that, once you get the family profile and see the drinking that goes on within it, could be attributed to FAS or FAE," says Elaine.

Beaudreau is described as a "vivid, articulate Lakota, a longtime resident of Pine Ridge who received her college and graduate degrees at St. Scholastica and Wyoming," according to Dorris. "She radiated authority, self-assuredness," he says. She told him that "we probably have two or three generations of FAE people," and when she says that various groups are trying to "change the tribal codes" to deal with the problems, he muses as follows:

This issue inevitably seemed to return to law, to external coercion in the absence of self-restraint, to a deprivation of liberty as a last resort. Again and again the people to whom I've talked, especially those on the front lines, face to face with the innocent victims of maternal drinking, came to the sorry conclusion that no arbitrary freedom was worth the cost in lives that FAS entailed. "Do unto others as you would have them do unto you" instructs the most elemental commandment of social intercourse. That is the rule, the "categorical imperative," as Immanuel Kant termed it, at the base of all cultures. It is the necessary condition for survival, but perhaps in its subtle permutations it is not part of our natural instinct; perhaps it must be imposed. *When that primal impulse does not flow of its own accord, laws have been written to mandate it.*

The cycle of alcohol abuse, Dorris claims, would be "almost impossible to interrupt through ordinary means." Sterilization is discussed as a last-ditch solution. Anyone who reads the compelling pages of this book knows that what happened to this innocent child is a heartbreaking tragedy, not only for the child but for his adoptive parents, an event in modern American society that occurs over and over again. But it also breaks your heart that Adam will never know the love of his Lakota mother, the acceptance of his blood relatives; that he will walk alone the streets of the cities of New Hampshire, live and work in a bowling alley far away from the Dakota prairie where he was born and where even now the birds are "bunching up," getting ready to leave, and the snow, in a few short weeks, will cover the tall, brittle grass; a place that apparently holds little charm for Dorris, who calls it "empty and harsh."

It is sad that Adam disappoints his adoptive parents every day of his existence, an interminable legacy that most of us, even those of us who are well and whole, would find unbearable. "Adam's birthdays are reminders for me," says Dorris. "For each celebration commemorating that he was born, there is the pang, the rage, that he was not born whole." Adam will face the grief of his adoptive parents for the rest of his life. Saddest of all, though, is the condemnation of his blood mother by his adoptive parents, their slandering of the young Lakota woman who bore him under what we may imagine as the most vile of human conditions.

As I read Dorris's work, I wanted somehow, in some small way—wanted to speak for her. I have no right to do so. I know nothing of the circumstances of her life. But there is one thing I am sure of . . . *someone must speak for her.*

She, too, has rights as a part of the human family, no matter how unworthy she is declared to be by others, and these rights are compelling. Civil rights. Human rights. She, too, as a creation of the Great Spirit, deserved love, supportive parents, a chance to live, though she never had any of it. Most of all, she should have had the right to speak for herself rather than to be condemned in history forever, maligned and threatened by those of us who now come from privileged worlds of scholarship, writers of theses and scholarly dissertations, graduates of Georgetown University, Yale, Dartmouth, the Ivy League places where success is assumed and unimagined access is the reward.

As Adam becomes twenty-one and faces his own life in an employment training program rather than the graduate program at Yale, which his adoptive father can't help but wish for him, his blood mother is called the *"original sinner,"* charged with committing the monstrous crime against Adam "in ignorance or wanton carelessness"—none of us knows which.

Like the people who blame homosexuals for AIDS and blame fourteen-year-old urban gang members for keeping the Medallín drug lords in Mercedes-Benzes, Dorris directs his frustrated wrath toward some of the least powerful among us: young childbearing Indian women. He says they must pay the price for the health crisis and family disintegration that can be observed not only on Indian reservations but in cities and rural areas throughout the country. Forcing these young women, as much the victims as their martyred children, into detention centers is presented as a solution to failed health care systems, inadequate education, poverty, and neglect. I thought we had learned from history that we could not legislate people into approved behavior.

Dorris's story obscures some very significant facts, if we are seriously looking for long-range solutions. A culture-based therapy model has been devised in Sioux Country in the last decade or so, and a young Lakota man by the name of Gene Thin Elk, who was raised between White River and Mission, South Dakota, is finding broad, enthusiastic, and hungry audiences for his methods. He is now based at the University of South Dakota in Vermillion, and he is easy to contact if anyone seriously wants to inquire about the holistic approach to finding answers to the alcoholism issues facing the Sioux. After I read *The Broken Cord*, I telephoned Thin Elk to see whether or not he had been interviewed by Dorris. He had not.

I can think of no reason for this omission. A culture-based therapy model such as Thin Elk's, recognizes that a significant revitalization of cultural ideals must be undertaken. Lakota/Dakota males must be part of the solution, for they possess great power in Sioux life; brothers, grandmothers, aunts and uncles, and fathers and sisters all have a role to play and a responsibility in all tribal crises, and especially in this one. In such a model we recognize that we cannot attack the young childbearing female as though she exists in a vacuum, nor can we call in the tribal police to restore what has been lost.

When Dorris looks at children at Project Phoenix and sees in them Adam's characteristics, he says, "I thought of the resources that have been available to Adam. . . . Harvard trained specialists, a university medical center . . . and what little impact they have made upon his life after years of concerted effort," and then he poses the following question: "Would, in fact, his long-term prognosis have been radically different if . . . Louise and I had never entered the picture?" The various responses to that query loom large.

Indeed, the adoption of Sioux children by those outside of the specific tribal perspective breaks one of the first rules of tribal sovereignty, and it was a much-deplored activity that brought about the 1978 passage of the Indian Child Welfare Act just a few years after Dorris took Adam into his home. One of the tenets of the Indian Child Welfare Act is that Indian relatives must be responsible to one another within a tribal context, and funding must be made available to build appropriate institutions on reservation lands so that this responsibility may be realized.

Are such children better off when they are taken into homes far away from their relatives and their places of birth? How is the Indian Child Welfare Act being implemented on reservations? How does the Dorris study strengthen the intent of the Indian Child Welfare Act? Or does it? What about the fact that Indian communities deplore the taking of their children because it neither allows nor forces the tribe to solve its problems of family chaos in appropriate ways? What about Adam's tribal identity? Does his mental retardation render that question moot?

What is the value of such a book as *The Broken Cord* to the Sioux tribes or to any tribes? Is it from such a book that we may glean little bits of information that we might be able to use as part of the solution? I would like to think so, but as I study it carefully, I am not convinced.

What is it that motivates a parent/scholar/writer to exploit the life of his child? Grief? Disappointment? A child's permission? Are there academic inquiries in Native American Studies that override a child's right to privacy? I know of no other Native American scholar who for public recognition or cause has so "used" his adoptive relatives, a ploy we have often criticized as ordinarily reserved for non-Indian anthropologists and researchers. Is there a moral violation of the parent-child relationship here that we in Indian Studies might find offensive?

One of the final questions to be asked is this: What kind of scholarship is useful to Indian communities, and how is it that *The Broken Cord* may be evaluated ultimately by those of us who are professionals in the field? It is the Indian Studies view that research is the component of the field that will ultimately allow us to revitalize ourselves as Indian nations of people and transcend the reactionary, defensive stance that has been so much a part of our academic and real-life experiences. In the light of that position, is *The Broken Cord* a responsible work? I think not.

I'm tempted to quip in a poorly imitated Bentsen/Quail replay: Michael Dorris, you're no Vine Deloria. But, frankly, that is too flippant an attitude toward a book as potentially explosive as this, a book of the sort that causes reactionary legislation toward Indian communities and Indian women in particular if it is taken seriously; a work that cannot be clearly defined generically and therefore remains ambiguous in purpose. Is it research? Is it autobiography? Is it polemic? Is it just a popularized pseudoanthropological work which can give grist to the James Clifford/Clifford Geertz controversy over the nature of ethnography in the modern world? Would it make a good television miniseries? What is this author's intent?[1]

His wife says, in the foreword "What I know my husband hopes for, in offering *The Broken Cord*, is a future in which this particular and preventable tragedy (FAS and FAE) will not exist." Such a hope misses its mark if it does not acknowledge and act upon the compassionate belief that Indian women do not, alone, bear the consequences of history, that *Lakota womanhood is also sacred*, and that Adam's mother, who deserved better from all of us, was as much a victim as her "friendly" child.

3

Black Eagle Child

Occasionally, but not often, I review a book that I consider flawless. This was one of those occasions.

As though intermediation could be the answer to the lack of written texts in the American Indian literary tradition, William Jones, at the turn of the century, wrote "The Culture Hero Myths of the Sauk and Foxes," a turgid, boring rendition of otherwise fascinating Mesquakie stories which appeared in the *Journal of American Folklore*. Such work absorbed the interest of a reading public and the scholarly world in such aggressive and oppressive ways that it became one of the fore-runners of a whole body of as-told-to autobiographical works that has since then become a generic core of "classics" used in the teaching of Native American literatures. Even *Black Elk Speaks*, *The Sixth Grandfather*, *Autobiography of a Winnebago Indian*, and other books owe their presence to such origins.

Now, upon the publication of the new prose work of the seasoned Mesquakie poet, Ray A. Young Bear, we find out what we might have suspected all along, that there is not even a passing resemblance in such William Jones translations, nor in any of the others, to the real voice of the native. If Ray Young Bear is starting a new trend, and I believe he is, such autobiographical works as his *Black Eagle Child: The Facepaint Narratives* may make the stodgy, Euroamerican, translated folkloric tradition and the genre of as-told-to life stories forever obsolete.

For the first time, we encounter an articulate, bilingual, tribal Phae-drus wrestling with his imperfect life vis-à-vis his own value system without the intervention of a Christian monitor or omniscient literary interpreter, and it is an inspiring event. In two languages Young Bear asks the questions about values to which there are no easy answers. What is good? What is bad? What happens to old values in a changing world? Is it possible to live a moral, ethical life? Like a tribal Robert M. Pirsig, he embarks on his own imprudent philosophical exploration of the world, the tribal/white world into which he was born, but he does it without benefit of a motorcycle analogy. No sailboat. No Zen. No organized religious thought unless you want to count the Well-Off Man Church, a name which amuses Young Bear as much as it does his readers. Mostly, it's just personal experience and tribal history, geography, and the sacred myths of one of the most remarkable tribal cultures ever to emerge and be sustained in the middle plains.

In 1965, Edgar Bearchild (Young Bear's autobiographical self) is still hanging around Why Cheer High School with Ted Facepaint ("a composite of a dozen people met, known, and lost in the last forty years") hoping "like persistent fools" for an invitation they can't refuse, but when it doesn't come, they join, instead, a gathering of peyotists at Circles-Back's house where Edgar, his eyeglasses fogged up and a lump in his throat, is overcome by a "sense of giddiness," ("I was never a good imitator"), and the impenitent Facepaint simply snores, farts, and winks unrestrainedly. Afterwards, life goes predictably on, and soon, under "the threat of permanent expulsion from the Why Cheer School District," Bearchild, suitcase in hand, hitchhikes out of Black Eagle Child Settlement to seize his future in "college prep classes for academically deprived minorities in northeastern Iowa." The struggle to become a writer begins, and Bearchild's grappling with questions of tribal concern in a changing world takes on substance:

With the gradual acceptance of modern change, fate dictated we would lose some aspects of our nefarious religion. We never accepted it, however. We led on proudly on the exterior, never quite knowing the masks of our fabulous lives were transparent, revealing to one and all that our insides were in disarray. Change was unavoidable; yet we blamed ourselves for creating new mythologies and rituals from the last traces of the old stories, our grandfathers' ways.

I stood and witnessed in awe. When blame was no longer applicable within the structure, fathers openly wept during their prayers, they brought news of insubordinate sons, the next leaders, to the masses. Being young I could not ascertain what was wrong or right, whether I as a son was responsible for fate itself. To me, the Spirits were ever-present regardless of ceremony. They and no one else decided. Could they not forgive? Or was that a Western concept? It had to be, thanks to Bible school I attended for three years as a child under Grandmother's encouragement. I was told Jesus Christ will always wait and forgive and forget one's misgivings. But George Whirlwind Boy said otherwise: "Our Principal Religion can never wait until you, yourself, decide the time is appropriate to believe and pray. That type of attitude is almost disrespectful. It has to be a lifetime commitment, not a momentary whim like that of the white man." *A wi t i ni ne ne ta qwa te sa ni ke tti ma ma to mo ne ni wi ya ni.* Perhaps it was not predetermined that I be an accomplished man of religion.

The quest broadens: if not a religious man, then, perhaps one with a realized sense of social consciousness. Not for many years has anyone really understood the political factions of the Mesquakie tribal world, but a maturing Young Bear, representing his family's legacy as well as Everyman's tribal voice, knows better than most that poking fun at the "lineage" abbreviations, which sometimes "got out of hand" (p. 98), is a tribal obligation, and he tells us why: "We sought and expected a grain of civility in our people," he says with a straight face, "regardless of who they were, i.e., an EBNO (enrolled but in name only), an EBNAR (enrolled but not a resident), BRYPU (blood-related yet paternally unclaimed), UBENOB (unrelated by either name or blood), EBMIW (enrolled but mother is white)." Chippewa writer Gerald Vizenor, long removed from real life on the homelands, regards this blood quantum as lunacy; his hero in *Heirs of Columbus* (1991) says Indians are "forever divided by the racist arithmetic measures of tribal blood," and young Bear gives it a reality check almost every reservation Indian has come to expect.

A mixture of the absurd and the serious is reflected in the chapter headings: "The Ugliest Man in Big Valley," "A Circus Acrobat on the Grass," "The Introduction of Grape Jell-O," "Alfred E. Neuman was an Arsonist." Like stills from *The Last Picture Show*, images of Precocious Charlotte, the Ontarios, and Zuni Indians sitting in candlelight are forever in Young Bear's memory; Hector Reveres Nothing does not come back from Vietnam; homey letters from Clotelde, and, finally, a decade after the Greyhound took him into a journey of understanding, the stunning news of a first fellowship and his acceptance into the literati.

Bearchild settles down with Selene Buffalo Husband, and the story continues. From what he has told us, we may be assured that in his newfound recognition of self, he will not, like another midwestern storyteller, Garrison Keillor, move to New York and sing in the Hopeful Gospel Quartet. Instead he will be with Selene, "on the hills overlooking the rivers." He will write down some of their songs "for the sake of remembering," and he will accept the answer to his quest: "There has to be a subtle transference of bigotry in the genes from one Why Cheer Generation to the next."

Finally, when a latter-day Facepaint appears at his door and says, ironically, "I need food, man," Bearchild, in a haunting Kafka-like drama recognizable to anyone who has ever taken seriously the putting of words on a blank piece of paper, describes his own writer's tragedy:

The long arduous task of pasting paper to every inch of my body had already begun and all that remained was the wait for it to set like a cocoon. I figured a metamorphosis was my only salvation.

Once the sunlight entered the bedroom, Selene had agreed to spin me as I hung from the ceiling like a giant piñata.

Inside the paper cocoon I was terribly alone, I could only imagine Selene's blistered hands turning me gently to dry. In the blindness the words from my childhood and past alighted on my sluggish tongue. Limited by space I could only transpose one or two words to a page with a short, dull pencil. Memorization was essential, and when it failed, I started the sentences over again. One day, having spent countless Big Chief tablets on "The Bread Factory" poem, I proclaimed myself the King of Revision. Believing it was a revelation and a half, I relayed it through a copper tube like a projectile from an Amazonian blowgun. Selene returned a note: "Underestimation of one's abilities can be a good thing." At last I was able to document my feeble beginning. Childhood was a precious epoch. Contrary to the beliefs of many, there was indeed a past.

Black Eagle Child: The Facepaint Narratives is an ambitious work from an accomplished writer who is dizzyingly complex, hostile and prickly, charming, weird, and brilliant. It marks the start of a revolution in tribal storytelling. It is a wise, impressive work as excessive in its honesty as it is in its optimism. No one, absolutely no one, tells the tribal story like Young Bear.

4

Black Hills, White Justice

Works which directly affect the political well-being of the Sioux Nation are, naturally, given priority for examination. Black Hills, White Justice *is one such work.*

Of special interest in the year of Columbus (the quincentenary of the discovery of America) is any text which intends to cast light upon the life, experience, and present state of the indigenes he is supposed to have discovered. Many Anglophiles, from fiction writer Mark Twain, who held stereotypic notions about the "free life" at a time when Americans knew it was over for them, to the French scholar, Alexis de Toqueville, who saw the Cherokee as inevitably "sad" and "displaced," have engaged in the instruction of the public on what America thinks about its colonial past. Now, attorney-turned-writer Edward Lazarus joins the fray.

To anyone who knows about the century-long fight of the Sioux Nation for its homelands in the northern plains, a book with the ironic title *Black Hills, White Justice* suggests an attempt to remind America of the paradoxical nature of its past; that is, that the controlling and liberating of the indigenes, the ideas about "justice for all" in one of the great democracies of any age, and the fairness of the American legal system vis-à-vis Indian policy may be failed ideals at best and a sham/racist policy at worst. Sadly, this book turns out to be a son's defense of his father's battered legal career in the Indian Claims Courts of the land. A more appropriate title might be *Lazarus's-Second Rise from the Dead*, for the author's father Arthur Lazarus, Jr., latter-day counsel to the Sioux and supposed heir to the Felix Cohen legacy of commitment to justice for Native America, stands accused since 1980 by the Sioux tribes of selling out the longest-running Indian claims case in the history of the United States, taking his ten-million-dollar fee from the huge judgment monies which the Sioux have refused to touch, and of violating one of

21

the most forgotten tenets of the law: that a lawyer, under the best of conditions and the worst (and especially if the client is innocent), must behave as though he believes in his client's legitimacy.

The agenda of this book, then, in spite of the author's disclaimers, serve several purposes: to justify the lawyer's arbitrary acceptance of the judgment monies over the client's objection; to press, belatedly, for that tribally rejected solution as the only logical and pragmatic thing to do, to legitimize the U. S. Claims Commission's principle (though it was apparently not the U. S. Congressional principle when Iraq stole Kuwait's land in 1991) that *Indian land acquired by theft cannot be returned to its original owners*; and, most offensive of all, that white lawyers know what is best for their "blind" Indian clients and that Arthur Lazarus, Jr., in particular, knows best and is therefore legitimate heir to Felix Cohen's long legal career in American Indian law.

Like his father and all of the white lawyers the Sioux have ever known, Edward Lazarus believes that the Sioux are a "conquered people" rather than the indigenes of the northern plains who have significant rights which must be articulated in the courtrooms of America. Because the Sioux are seen as a defeated people, lawyers engage in promoting merely pragmatic solutions rather than ethical ones. Here is an example:

Early in the spring of 1979, at the request of Gonzalez [an Oglala attorney from Pine Ridge, S.D.] Lazarus traveled to Pine Ridge to explain at an open meeting the status of the Black Hills claim and in particular his continued pursuit of a money judgment. Confronting a boisterous and hostile crowd, Lazarus tried again to explain what was possible under the white man's system and urged the Sioux to pursue *the best possible result* that his system would provide. He tried again to explain that while "The Black Hills Are Not For Sale" (which is earlier dismissed by the author as an "innocuous resolution" passed by the Oglala Tribal Council) might be an attractive political slogan, it had no real meaning in the legal world.

This epitomizes the conflicting issues which Edward Lazarus attempts to define in his father's favor. It sets up an agenda for the final chapters of the book which results in the arrogant condemnation of the positions of resistance taken by the Lakota/Dakota people toward this matter, accounting for the author's contempt for Sioux leadership, which he reveals throughout the manuscript. Some of the most disturbing suggestions of the book are that the Sioux were "blind and mute and utterly dependent," that "defining legal strategies lay beyond their ken," that the Black Hills Nation Council is simply a "self-promoting organization," that spokespersons (in this case the renowned Yankton

Sioux lawyer Ramon Roubideaux, who has probably won more civil and criminal cases for the people than any other lawyer in the northern plains) can be labeled as representing just "another Sioux faction," that Lazarus's "untutored clients could not help him," and, astonishingly, "that the theory of sovereignty was unknown to the Sioux," traditionally. These suggestions, apparently, are intended to promote the idea that Lazarus and Sonosky Law Offices came out to Sioux Country and saved the Indians, not only from a corrupt legal strategy in the claims process, but from themselves. Throughout the text, Lazarus uses examples of the political wranglings of the Sioux (an eye-opening activity that no one who has ever attended a Sioux political meeting would think of denying, but, significantly, a trait of all dynamic, democratic societies) as evidence to discredit them as leaders of their own people and shapers of their own policy. About tribal governments, he says that the "U. S. Government has poured millions into reservations with little or nothing to show for it."

In what psychologists might call a "passive-aggressive" manner, author Lazarus takes to task the young Oglala Sioux lawyer, Mario Gonzalez (who probably did more to get the Sioux claims matters on track than anyone in the last century), saying that Gonzalez's theories were and are simply wrong, that he engaged in activities "endangering the tribe's new lawsuit," and that through these activities he was giving the Sioux people "false hope." No doubt what prompts this assessment of the Indian lawyer's work, which in some cases Lazarus seems to admire, is that Gonzalez said publicly what the Sioux were saying privately: "It is inappropriate for Mr. Lazarus to collect this huge fee for misconduct." Indeed, it is the position of many of the Sioux people who attended a meeting which this reviewer attended at the Mother Butler Center in Rapid City in October, 1991, that it might be immoral for the writer/lawyer/son to return and make more money by writing the book and continuing to misrepresent them. A Sioux Indian from the audience asked, "Aren't you ashamed to come back for a second helping?"

Gonzalez and other Sioux politicians, scholars, and leaders have become in the last decade the shapers of new policies and theories toward the appropriate solution of the Black Hills claims matter, but Lazarus' account in *Black Hills, White Justice* does not appropriately assess the work that has been done by the Sioux in defense of the lands. The fact is that if Gonzalez had not at the right moment in the litigation filed for an injunction on behalf of the Oglalas to prevent the Secretary of the Interior from paying the $106 million (to its collaborator, the BIA), the entire claim would have been lost to Lazarus's giant sell-out. Yet, Gonzalez is dismissed in this book as merely a descendent of "one of the first *agitators*," and, in its final pages, the Sioux themselves are slandered as having "abandoned any meaningful attempt to control their own destiny in favor of *rhetorical* claims to sovereignty and independence." The claims process says Lazarus, "has encouraged them to evade any real responsibility for repairing the tragic condition of their lives."

All of this vicious assessment of the Sioux, both as individuals and as a nation of people by Lazarus in an attempt to repair his father's career as legal counsel to the tribes has obscured some of the very interesting and useful research that has gone into the manuscript. Ignoring the obvious errors like the photo of a Navajo woman captioned "Sioux Reservation Life, 1936, Charlotte Lloyd (Westwood) Walkup," and the fact that he names Oliver Red Cloud instead of Royal Bull Bear as head of the Grey Eagles Society, some of Lazarus's assessment of the earlier litigation process, such as the inadequacies of the work by legal advisor and former South Dakota Senator Ralph Case, as well as the damaging influence of historical congressional policy, proves useful. This case has been in the courts, after all, since 1920, and carries with it considerable historical baggage. Such documentation shows the author's sincere effort to produce a work of scholarship which he says he hopes can help to broaden what he sees to be a "window of opportunity" for the Sioux in their efforts.

"The American people have a soft spot for Indians," he told this reviewer, revealing his shallow understanding of this Indian/white conflict which plagues America. There is no better time than now, he believes, for the Sioux to take their "judgment" monies, mount a huge public relations campaign, and try to win back their lands. The key word in that phrase is, I think, *try*. In this final ironic, sad, and failed counsel to the Sioux, he tells them that the money "can be used as a political weapon."

This is a book which will provide the easy way out; indeed, it is the ultimate "buy-out" of an act of criminal expansionist U. S. historical behavior articulated by those who do not understand that federal Indian policy and law is an *evolving* process. If justice for Indians has not been attained through the courts and political processes, as Lazarus suggests, it is appropriate for all of us who dare to plunge into the treacherous history of *Black Hills, White Justice* to continue to believe in justice as an American ideal, which will lead us to seek new methods for rendering justice to America's first nations, not to capitulate to more failed solutions. That capitulation is, unfortunately, embedded in one of the arguments put forth in Arthur Lazarus, Jr.'s "Brief for the Sioux Nation," during the October term of the Supreme Court of the United States in 1979: "Indian tribes are entitled to the same measure of just compensation for the taking of their property by the United States as any other landowner." Indian tribes, of course, are not like any other American landowners. They are sovereign, separate, and distinct peoples, with signed treaty rights, and more work needs to be done to articulate that idea on behalf of the indigenes.

Black Hills, White Justice claims to elucidate the ethical, moral questions posed by the Sioux Black Hills case, yet comes to an immoral, unethical conclusion. What is even more disappointing is that this privileged, wealthy American writer/lawyer (who "listened to this story at the dinner table" throughout his younger years) fails to tell his readers that the return of homelands to the Sioux Nation is possible, that the return of the Sioux lands can be accomplished in this century with very minimal upheaval, that the Sioux defenders of their lands are intelligent, thoughtful, realistic people who understand their own political, historical, and spiritual condition, and that they are right in their resistance and will eventually be strengthened by it.

Though Lazarus rejects the hope that Americans have the will for a fair settlement of this case, which means the return of lands, the Sioux continue to believe in the potential for American justice and, at this moment at least, do not seem to be giving up their demands for land reform in the Black Hills. The Sioux go about their lives on eight reserved homelands in North and South Dakota in spite of what Lazarus's hopeless vision of the Sioux tells him and his oftentimes uninformed audiences: "And, in the meantime, of Red Cloud's seven generations, four already have died. The fifth is dying now." In this puzzling accounting of historical eras, he apparently fails to grasp the notions about mortality which apply to all of us: that the past four generations of his own people have died, also. It is obvious that he did not accompany Arvol Looking Horse and the Big Foot Riders, either spiritually or physically, as they rode from Fort Yates, North Dakota, to Wounded Knee, South Dakota, in 1990 to heal the Sioux Nation's hoop. Had he done so, he might not dismiss such histories as "rhetorical," nor would he say that the Sioux "perhaps reflect an incipient sense of sovereignty or nationhood."

Anyone who reads history knows that the Sioux have been declared dead and dying by many writers and scholars more prestigious than Edward Lazarus. Such death knells for the indigenes are the very philosophical bases of much American thought, vain hopes and forecasts which permeate the work of many legal scholars and intellectuals of all disciplines.

What is sadly missing from this scholarship and from Lazarus's work, in particular, is an understanding of the warrior spirit of Oyate. Also missing is the faith that America can live up to its ideals.

Part Two

DISPOSSESSION

5

Why I Can't Read Wallace Stegner

The invasion of North America by European peoples has been portrayed in history and literature as a benign movement directed by God, a movement of moral courage and physical endurance, a victory for all humanity. As the face of Europe (as well as Asia and Africa) changes at the close of the twentieth century, this portrayal of colonialism and its impact on the unfortunate Indians who possessed the continent for thousands of years before the birth of America, seems to go unchallenged either in politics or letters by most mainstream thinkers. It arrives in academia unscathed, to be spoonfed to future generations.

Few writers of fiction so eloquently and un-self-consciously examined this portrayal as did Wallace Stegner, the novelist and essayist who saw himself as "native" to the Dakota states, to Iowa, the Montana and Canadian border country, that is, the northern plains. "If I am native to anything, I am native to this," he said of the Cypress Hills country of Canada. Having written twelve novels and seven nonfiction works, as well as countless articles and reviews, and as the recipient of the 1971 Pulitzer Prize, a Senior Fellowship from the NEH, and numerous other prestigious awards, he was and is considered a major American literary figure and precursor to the many contemporary and lesser luminaries who write on Western history and literature.[1]

This acclaimed body of work by one of the giants of American letters expresses his point of view that "[W]estern history sort of stopped at 1890," thus representing the continuum of optimism concerning the survival of a civilization based upon its fondly remembered colonial past. There is, perhaps, no American fiction writer who has been more successful in serving the interests of a nation's fantasy about itself than Wallace Stegner, and there are few of us who have not read his works.

The experiences of Stegner are those of a vast portion of the American public. His experiences, one supposes, are broadly accepted as the

29

events and feelings known to second-, third-, and fourth-generation European immigrants to the land. As they did, Stegner simply claims indigenousness and begins to set down the new myths and stories of those newcomers stepping off boats and, in the process, continues the personalization of history and setting that is so dear to the hearts of the so-called regional American writers. This personalization takes place in the imagination, thus the claim to identity needs only acclamation. When Stegner uses "wolf willow," then, as an example of how it is that a particular environment is remembered, he creates it as archetypal metaphor emblematic of how humans may begin to understand the function of what T. S. Eliot has called the "collective unconscious."

It is human nature to be moved by the possibility that such mechanisms work universally and because of that, the substance of what Stegner imagines becomes believable to everyone except those who have had thousands of years of prior knowledge of that same world and environment and imagined it on their own very different terms. Stegner's imagination of the West, which declares that in 1890 a world ended, is of course not his own invention. As noted by historians of his time, that world had significance somewhere in the past but, apparently, not in the present, nor in the future. Stegner and Indians, then, are (no pun intended) worlds apart. He simply took them as his culture gave them to him, though it is possible for those of us who read his works to wonder whether or not he grasped the final immorality of such a position.

Because I am an Indian, born and raised on a northern plains Indian reservation in this century, I argue with Stegner's reality. The culture I have known imagines a different continuity and intimacy with the universe, which in large part still exists. It exists in communities all over the region, in language and myth, and in the memories of people who know who they are and where they came from. Unless someone comes forward to say that Western history did not stop in 1890, Indians will forever be exempted from Descartes's admonition concerning humanity: "I think, therefore, I am." Worse yet, fraudulent public policy toward Indians has been and is even now imposed through the conversionary use of imagined realities.

It seems important, then, to call for a shift in attitude concerning the history and literature of the region called the West. As a Dakotah writer, I am hostile to the idea that history stopped in 1890, the year of the massacre at Wounded Knee of hundreds of Minneconjous in a place which was destined to become the State of South Dakota, because in the imagination of the Sioux, that moment of awful violence has meant the beginning of hard times, the basis for evidence of a long and glorious history, the focal point of survival.

These days, a century after what is said by Stegner to be a death notice, Sioux relatives and Indians from across the land have called for a full apology from the U. S. government and payment of reparations for the undeserved death of Indians who had signed a peace treaty and carried the white flag as they traveled through their own country on that fateful December day. It is not likely that these requests will be met any time soon, but Indians everywhere understand the resistance to them. They are not unaware that the easiest solution to a problem of such magnitude, which reveals four hundred years of a corruptly imagined world, is to do one of two things: either maintain silence or feign ignorance. Indians everywhere know how important this standoff is, because there is a tacit understanding that reparations and apologies are awarded to peoples who continue to exist—the Japanese who survived World War II, for example, or the Jews who survived the Nazi Holocaust.

Since Stegner wrote of a sorrowful past as it concerned Indians, his work has served to give regional and American literature of the West a cloak of respectability. Not unlike the U. S. Congress, which has expressed regret for the tragedy of Wounded Knee in 1890, Stegner expressed for all of America, in his conversation with Etulain and in *Wolf Willow*, that his people believed "this country was a new country, and a new country had no history," that "the world when I began to know it had neither location nor time, geography, nor history." Claiming ignorance, Stegner can say that the final curtain has fallen, no handprints of any human perpetrator can be found, criminal action requires no reprimand. The concern for all of us who put pen to paper should be that such a position has the potential to cut off dialogue and condemn to oblivion or absurdity Indian writers who want to continue the drama.

Stegner lamented, "Education tried, inadequately and hopelessly, to make a European out of me," ironically and sadly disposing of the only legitimate legacy he and other immigrant children could claim. Like other Americans, he cried, "I wish our homes and schools had given us our history"; "I wish I had seen . . ."; "We were not informed in school . . ."; "I wish I had heard of the coming of the Sioux"; and "I wish I had known . . ." as though there is nothing that could be done about the past. The principal perpetrators of a wrongful history, as far as Stegner was concerned, are allowed to melt into the heroic and hopeful future of America with no more than an expression of regret.

Such terrible regret is expressed so beautifully that readers are helpless to resist a sympathetic emotional response. This is the power of Stegner and those who preceded him, and of those American writers of the West who follow. They all become part of the American literary movement which claims possession of the American West. In the process, they become teachers, researchers, interpreters, historians. Un-self-consciously, they write about the plains and the American Indian and their own experiences in an attempt to clarify their own identities. Yet, in a moment of schizophrenia so appropriate to anyone who continually withdraws from reality, Stegner claims an affinity with Indians by calling himself "a sensuous little savage," not a child of Europe.

"Living in Cypress Hills, I did not even know I lived there and hadn't the faintest notion of who lived there before me," he admitted, in *Wolf Willow* and as he uttered this ignorance he spoke for all immigrant and pioneer offspring of America. Following this terrible admission and the information that he left there never to return, living some fifty-odd years elsewhere, he gave prominence to the idea that indigenousness was for those who claimed it. His attitude toward what he saw as the ignorance and omission of his ancestors with regard to history was accepting, sympathetic, quite without malice, and compassionate.

In his misunderstanding and dismissal of indigenousness and his belief in the theory that American Indians were "vanishing" he was much like writers everywhere who offer only a narrowness of vision and a confused history. Following a compelling description of the Sioux Chieftain Sitting Bull's return to the United States from his Canadian exile at the close of the nineteenth century, Stegner said, as so many American writers and historians had said before him, "The Plains Indians were done."

He does not say how this could be so in the face of evidence that representatives of Plains Indian nations signed peace treaties with the United States federal government, reserved land bases and rights for themselves and their future generations, and set up governments which continued to adapt to the inevitable changes of the modern world.

He does not say how this could be so when native populations exist all over the American landscape, identified by cartographers as occupying space on maps, by linguists as speaking hundreds of languages; people who have been reenacting their own mythologies at significant moments, cherishing the desire to sundance in the summer sun at Devil's Tower, Wyoming, and to pray with the pipe at Green Grass, South Dakota. These people who continue to reproduce themselves biologically and tell their children to whom they are related cannot be wished away either through the deception of the imagination or by any other distractions which are probably more political than artistic.

The lack of credibility of Stegner's dismissal of the Plains Indians is tolerable only because Stegner wrote for an audience made up of the children and offspring of pioneer settlers, the one or two of every four Americans who trace their ancestry to the immigrants and European colonizers of this American soil. This is a large audience.

Even though Stegner says that "education tried, inadequately and hopelessly to make a European of me," quite the opposite seems to be true. As he writes the history of the plains and claims that the Plains Indians were done, he reiterates the belief and hope of those European immigrants who created an acceptable past for Americans who continue to occupy the territory of the northern plains today. Stegner's attitude is, without question, the pervasive attitude of white midwesterners whose ancestors marched into a moral void and then created through sheer will the morality that allowed them, much the same way that the contemporary white Dutch South Africans marched into South Africa proclaiming Pretoria, to convince the world that "this is my country."

Isolated from this behavior and history, declared "done" and "vanished," the American Indian has little right to hope, since the forming of a dialectic apart from and independent of the direction of mass culture is often considered such a drastic departure as to be unscholarly. A contradictory question, however, must be asked: How may a contemporary American Indian reader of such fiction and history as Stegner's work about the American West reconcile his or her imagination of mythological continuity and primordial historiography with the death and burial of his or her presence made so explicit?

Quite frankly, I can think of no question more important to a writer and to a culture, especially since continued actions emerge from these imaginings, derived from place and history. Certainly, if the question is unasked, no answer can be forthcoming. While such a question and its answer may bring the unwelcome news that we have been enemies and perhaps still are, it is essential to self-knowledge, both individually and collectively, that we ask it. I can think of no question more vital as we enter into discussions with the new democrats at Prague and Warsaw, and as Chinese students in Tiananmen Square raise a replica of the Statue of Liberty.

It may be that Americans will have to come face to face with the loathsome idea that their invasion of the New World was never a movement of moral courage at all; rather, it was a pseudoreligious and corrupt socioeconomic movement for the possession of resources. It may be that the Plains Indians are not "done," as assumed in Stegner's fiction; rather, they continue to multiply and prosper. The threat of these two possibilities exposes the vision of a writer like Stegner to a different interpretation but does not necessarily make that vision fraudulent. Vision is vision, after all, a sacred thing, as all of the tribes will tell you. The hazardous nature of a vision of America grounded in disguised dogma rather than in human terms, however, if it does not make the Indian deny himself, makes him at the very least deny society.

An even more significant danger, though, is the fact that the resigned immigrant/colonist grandchild who remains tied historically and culturally to the purist's notion of the making of America as a morality play may, unfortunately, continue to exert the greatest influence on the taking of action in this country's political, social, and academic life that is inappropriate for the twenty-first century. This is not purely, as far as Indians are concerned at least, an academic issue, nor is it only a problem of simple idealism. It is a serious sociological and political matter in which legislation and social action are grounded.

Writers of fiction who become party to the declaration of Indian demise do so, usually, by being first of all misguided interpreters of what they and others so carefully observe and assiduously trace as American Indian behavior and belief. Stegner, for example, includes in *Wolf Willow* a chapter called "The Last of the Exterminators," a confusing discussion about values which he says started with Paul Sharp's *Whoop-Up Country*. He affirms Sharp's smug notion, which he presents as flawless truth, that "plains Indians generally regarded the theft of a horse from someone outside the tribe the way Americans regard the theft of home base."

This contrived explanation of the attitude and behavior of Plains Indians does little to help the reader truly understand how Plains Indians regarded horse stealing. There is probably little primary evidence, beyond this kind of fictional illusion, that Plains Indians did, indeed, regard horse theft as gamesmanship of this sort. To suggest such a cavalier attitude toward an important cultural survival tactic would be to reduce these matters to cliché. This kind of cliché is much like the revelatory dialogue so familiar to movie-goers, "It's a good day to die," shouted by the chief, his rifle raised above his head, as he rides pell-mell into enemy ranks. Surely, such absurd folks can be dismissed altogether as real, continuing, or thoughtful participants in any national discourse.

Clever prose style and substance in fiction as well as nonfiction interests the American reader as entertainment, but the purpose it ultimately serves is threatening. It serves to make the claim of the nativeness of all European immigrants to this land more valid because such indigenous populations as are described here will not last long, and if they do somehow survive their own ridiculousness, they will do so as degenerates of history, defeated and outrageous.

Even in this early work, Stegner's modernist trend in this same chapter becomes critical of the same American development he so respectfully defends in the interest of understanding the promise of democracy. He takes swipes at Canadian settlers and fur traders he calls the "wolfers," the Hudson Bay Company, and the American intrusion into the plains of Canada, contrasting the Canadian system of monopoly trading with Indians to the American system of "competition, whiskey, bullets, exploitation, and extermination." There is the suggestion here that Canada showed more interest in long-term cohabitation rather than a short-term exploitive relationship that it could establish with the natives of the land, an idea that was, from the point of view of contemporary knowledge and experience, more hopeful than actual.

Stegner's discussion of "class" society of the American plains is just as wrong-headed. His claim that the *metis* (French and Indian mixed-blood population) served as a "buffer race" and the "wolfers" as an "advancing fringe of civilization, an indispensable broom sweeping clean the plains for white occupation," is an idea which Indians find preposterous. They probably did not consider the metis as a buffer, nor the wolfers as civilized. Stegner considers them all "exterminators of their own kind."

The description of the metis, or half-breeds, as a buffer race, which means that they are "a small, neutral race or state lying between potentially hostile larger ones," is, in terms of their relationship to Indians, the beginning of a deception which allows the turning away from what was really happening in Indian communities. The metis would hardly have been called neutral by any of the plains peoples and societies for whom the arranged marriage patterns of ancient times were a tool of cultural survival. Instead, the metis were and probably still are seen by native peoples as those who were *already converts* to the hostile and intruding culture simply through their marriage into it. To say that they were neutral would mean that they were "not inclining toward or actively taking either side in a matter under dispute," and belonged "to neither side or part." With regard to their role in the enforced assimilation and oppression of native populations by the American and Canadian governments, both statements would be debatable.

Oral historians of Indian nations contend that the half-breed phenomenon was responsible for much hatred and violence within tribal groups. This was and still is especially true in the plains cultures, where it was clear from the beginning that the male person of the native society was being stripped of his power, his role in society, and his lands and possessions by the white man who married the tribal woman and eventually made what they considered chaotic principles of a new, nontraditional government possible. Few historians have really dealt with this matter, but many tribal leaders of the Plains Indians believed that the destruction of culture caused by the killing of the buffalo was no more and no less devastating than the destruction of culture caused by the dismissal of marriage patterns deriving from and supportive of the extended family (called *tiospaye* by the Sioux), so long protected by the tribes. To claim that a society which was produced through unsanctioned marriage and reproductive activities could be considered a buffer is to look at it from a purely European point of view, not from the vantage point of the *tiospaye* value system.

American Indian nations did not in history, nor do they today, view intermarriage as buffer, though some individuals may hold that position. For the most part, native populations continue to view intermarriage as one of the risks to cultural and political survival, and there is plenty of evidence in contemporary tribal life to indicate that the Plains Indians have always regarded it with suspicion. Native languages describe biological and cultural relationships of human beings to one another with great explicitness, and the half-breed phenomenon is held in quite tentative regard by native-language speakers. The Sioux still call those with white blood *iyeska*, literally translated as "talks white," and it is not generally regarded as a complimentary term.

The interpretation of day-to-day Indian/white relationships through the appropriation of imagined native response to historical events is another marvelously persuasive technique which writers like Stegner employ over and over again to gain authenticity. A clear example from Stegner is given in "The Law in a Red Coat," a seminal essay in which he romanticizes the Canadian Mountie.

The first member of the Royal Canadian Mounted Police (RCMP) Stegner ever laid eyes on became heroic. "I believe I know, having felt it, the truest reason why the slim force of Mounted Police was so spectacularly successful," Stegner said, "why its esprit de corps was so high and its prestige so great. I *think I know how law must have looked to the Sioux and Blackfoot* when the column of redcoats rode westward in the summer of 1874 [my italics]." He goes on to claim that in contrast to the American cavalry, which had become "an abomination to the Plains hostiles," the Red Coats' justice had meant "to Indian minds non- and sometimes anti-American," thus implying their virtue as perceived by Indians. Such imagining, reminiscent of Sherwood Anderson and

Damon Runyon, described "good" Canadian Mountie law, not "bad" American law, according to Stegner.

The idea that Indians as a group and more specifically those Indians who led their people to continued nationhood in spite of the bloody threat of extinction, would perceive the RCMP as substantially different from the U.S. Cavalry is, I think, an example of wishful thinking. *Colonial Law is always recognizable to the colonized!* Indians of today, for example, were not at all surprised to learn from the careful research done by Peter Matthiessen for his book *In the Spirit of Crazy Horse* that the RCMP, during the upheavals in South Dakota of the 1970s, falsified documents *in favor of the U. S. Government* in the Leonard Peltier extradition case, a fact which has been substantiated by further examination.[2]

A broader look at history might suggest that the idea that Indian hating was nonexistent and empire building less violent in Canada than in the United States is simply a delusion of the imagination. Racism and its relationship to colonization and nationbuilding on the North American continent seems fairly pervasive and consistent. For Stegner to exempt his beloved Canada is a combination of compelling fantasy and bad history.

It is important to say that the business of claiming indigenousness and inventing supportive mythology is an activity of the human imag- ination. No one argues that the declaration of one's identity is not an imaginative act. The Hopi and Dakotah, Navajo and Nez Perce have been in this business far longer than we know, certainly centuries prior to anything that Americans might have experienced. All imaginative writing and even nonfictional work defines truth and belief as the par- ticular writer knows it, otherwise it is simply fruitless activity. Stegner's imagination, then, and his obvious popularity with the American reader must not be condemned as fruitless. It is, rather, a valiant attempt at mythologizing one's relationship to place. No sensible storyteller of any age would put forth an argument denying the legitimacy and necessity of doing just that.

The distinct idiom of Stegner's imaginative writing as it applies to nativeness, as well as his work in nonfiction, however, suggests two troubling ideas concerning cultural nationalisms. First, if there is no challenge to the wrong-headed notion that Western history ended in 1890, its absence closes forever any further analysis of a period of time, and the result is that there will be no direction for new forms to take should they somehow manage to emerge. Second, the unchallenged statement that the Plains Indians are "done" forever excludes Indians from participation in the community of contemporary human thought.

This is recognized by readers of history as the political strategy of any imperialistic entity, but for it to be buried in the work of a major American fiction writer and not subject to analysis amounts to a lack of responsibility in literary studies.

If one is an *American* writer, neither of these ideas makes sense, for they embody the most characteristic European feature of the modern historical outlook—that as one nation rises, the other dies. This is the typical Anglo-Saxon historical view. Americanisms, on the other hand, are supposed to be "new-worldisms," setting off innovations of all kinds and allowing for the possibility that there are *living* resources in indigenous societies.

Unfortunately, Stegner's theory is that as America rises, the Sioux Nation expires. We need only to look at Lithuania, at Poland, Bulgaria, and other national groups involved in the reorganization of the former USSR in the 1990s to know that nations do not die simply because another nation has willed it so.

From the point of view of American Indians, the declaration of their demise (based on racial prejudices) has done much harm. Yet, the Stegner phenomenon of exclusivity in literature and history is powerful. It takes over, colonizes, invades the reality of human experience in North America to the extent that the concepts of *indigenousness* and *aboriginality* are quite misdefined and ultimately misunderstood by the reading public. When that happens, the American Indian's literary, historical, and cultural presence in America is repeatedly falsified or denied.

The underlying assumption that one world can begin only if another ends—life without continuity, humanity without history—is cause for great sadness, regret, and misery. I weep for Stegner when he says, "I saw the homestead just once after we left it to go back into town in the bitter fall of 1919. In the spring of 1920 we came past it on our way to Montana and camped in the shack for one night. We did not even take the boards off the windows or roll up the canvas blinds, but went about in the familiar, musty place, breathing the heavy air, in a kind of somnambulism. Our visit was not meant to change anything or restore for an instant the hope we had given up. *We merely passed through*, picked up a few objects that we wanted, touched things with our hands in a reminding way, stood looking from the doorway down across the coulee [my italics]."

Perhaps we can weep for all Americans who were and are *merely passing through*. But that does not mean we can excuse them for imagining and believing that American Indians, too, are or were *merely passing through*, a mere phase of history to be disclaimed or forgotten or, worse yet, nostalgically lamented. To do so is to misunderstand indigenousness and to appropriate the American Indian imagination in the same way the colonists appropriate the land and resources of the New World.

The results of such colonialistic imaginations are disastrous not only to Indians but, perhaps, to all the world. It is not merely that such imagination exemplified by Wallace Stegner amounts to the restructuring of a rather irksome historical experience with regard to Indians. It is not just that it is an unpleasant fact that new societies and new nations are born from the spilling of the blood of other nations—a fact that must be denied if a nation is to see itself as ethical. It is not just that American writers don't want to see the themselves as participants in a European colonial past and so create a vision which allows America a nationalistic role never before invented in the history of mankind: morally courageous, directed by God, acting as and for all humanity the new light of freedom everywhere. It is not just any of that. It is the realization that this mechanism will surely fail, for it is not the inherent right of any people to survive and rule because of an exclusive relationship with God.

The tyranny of expectation, then, comes into full play. The strength given this failed ethos by certain American literatures for whom Stegner is a major role player may be a fatal mistake—and not just for Indians. As the imagined America goes about in its disguise, its powerful economic system, capitalism, exploits resources for profit in a way which exempts native populations, its scientific mentality steals the sun and markets firepower to its friends, its "superior" governing class develops to deny religious, social and political freedoms to large groups of people. It will not be long before all mankind will believe that the tyrant must be overthrown. When that happens, it may be too late for contest, challenge, and debate.

Nothing that I have said suggests that the future will be easy, nor can we know that there is anything except hard work ahead. For now, though, I have to be content to simply encourage the new scholars and writers who have begun to understand what is at stake. For now I have to be content in my own realization that the partisan struggle in which I've been engaged will eventually matter. Indian Studies scholars who have been studying Indian histories and lifeways in the past two or three decades have been doing so for the purpose of petitioning for redresses of grievances in this democracy. In the process of that engagement they have helped everyone to understand that the need for transformation is urgent and compelling. I am certain that these partisan struggles will inspire those who believe they have an intuitive responsiblity to humanity. In the meantime, my reading in the works of Wallace Stegner is minimally undertaken and then only to remind myself that literature can and does successfully contribute to the politics of possession and dispossession.

6

A Centennial Minute from
Indian Country; or Lessons in
Christianizing the Aboriginal
Peoples of America
from the Example of
Bishop William Hobart Hare

On Tuesday, December 20, 1988, the following public declaration appeared in Indian newspapers. It was a year before the great centennial celebrations of the western states of America took place, a period which provided an appropriate mechanism for further discussion of the historical role of Christian churches in what some benignly label Indian-white relations, and others like myself choose to call Indian dispossession:

To The Tribal Councils and Traditional Spiritual Leaders of the Indian and Eskimo Peoples of the Pacific Northwest

Dear Brothers and Sisters,

This is a formal apology on behalf of our churches for their long-standing participation in the destruction of traditional Native American spiritual practices. We call upon our people for recognition of and respect for your traditional ways of life and for protection of your sacred places and ceremonial objects. We have frequently been unconscious and insensitive and have not come to your aid when you have been victimized by unjust Federal policies and practices. In many other circumstances we reflected the rampant racism and prejudice of the dominant culture with which we so willingly identified. During the 200th

41

Anniversary years of the United States Constitution we as leaders of our children in the Pacific Northwest, extend our apology. We ask for your forgiveness and blessing.

As the Creator continues to renew the earth, the plants, the animals and all living things, we call upon the people of our denominations and fellowship to a commitment of mutual support in your efforts to reclaim and protect the legacy of your own traditional spiritual teachings. To that end we pledge our support and assistance in upholding the American Religious Freedom Act (P. L. 95-134, 1978) and within that legal precedent affirm the following:

1) The rights of the Native Peoples to practice and participate in traditional ceremonies and rituals with the same protection offered all religions under the Constitution.

2) Access to and protection of sacred sites and public lands for ceremonial purposes.

3) The use of religious symbols (feathers, tobacco, sweet grass, bones, etc.) for use in traditional ceremonies and rituals.

The spiritual power of the land and the ancient wisdom of your indigenous religions can be, we believe, great gifts to the Christian churches. We offer our commitment to support you in the righting of previous wrongs: To protect your people's efforts to enhance Native spiritual teachings; to encourage the members of our churches to stand in solidarity with you on these important religious issues; to provide advocacy and mediation, when appropriate, for ongoing negotiations with State Agencies and Federal officials regarding these matters.

May the promises of this day go on public record with all the congregations of our communions and be communicated to the Native American Peoples of the Pacific Northwest. May the God of Abraham and Sarah, and the Spirit who lives in both the Cedar Salmon People be honored and celebrated.

Sincerely,

The Rev. Thomas L. Blevins, Bishop
Pacific Northwest Synod-Lutheran Church in America

The Rev. Dr. Robert Bradford, Executive Minister
American Baptist Churches of the Northwest

The Rev. Robert Brock
NW Regional Christian Church

The Right Rev. Robert H. Cochrane, Bishop
Episcopal Diocese of Olympia

The Rev. W. James Halfaker, Conference Minister
Washington-North Idaho Conference
United Church of Christ

The Most Rev. Raymond G. Hunthausen
Archbishop of Seattle
Roman Catholic Archdiocese of Seattle

The Rev. Elizabeth Knott, Synod Executive
Presbyterian Church Synod Alaska-Northwest

The Rev. Lowell Knutson, Bishop
North Pacific District, American Lutheran Church

The Most Rev. Thomas Murphy, Coadjutor
Archbishop Roman Catholic Archdiocese of Seattle

The Rev. Melvin G. Talbert, Bishop
United Methodist Church

The church's public apology gets much play in the media, while the important issues of the return of stolen lands for economic benefit to the Indian populations are never addressed. In the one hundredth year of statehood for many of the states of the west and the two hundredth year of the United States Constitution (and in a time when people looked forward to the 1992 celebration of the arrival of Columbus to these shores), this early centennial apology by the church leaders of the northwestern United States to the tribal leaders of the Indian and Eskimo peoples of the Pacific Northwest was to become a grand gesture in regional Christian Church history as a special gift to the tribes, a device of uncommon reconciliation and a tool for sharing the spirituality, culture, and concern for creation.

It would be one of many such reconciliation efforts which would mark the last decade of the century. In reality, however, it did nothing to return lands stolen from the tribes through century-long legislative fraud, nor did it affect the federal government's oppression of tribes, nor the criminal behavior of state governments and law enforcement entities illegally lodged on Indian homelands. Indeed, reconciliation efforts of this sort did little to change the racialized status quo inherent in Indian/white relations throughout the West. Since Christian churches were for two hundred years so successful in the destruction of native culture(s), the lack of power in their contemporary efforts to redeem themselves in terms of specific acts can only be viewed with open cynicism.

One way of understanding the church's current activity, however, is to read a seminal work called *The Image* by Daniel J. Boorstin, a history professor and former head of the Library of Congress. This is a book described as "very informative and entertaining and chastising" by *Harper's* magazine in 1961, and it helps us to identify the preceding public declaration by the church as what Boorstin calls a *pseudo-event*. Look at the following illustration by Boorstin of how this mechanism works in the modern world:

The owners of a hotel, in an illustration offered by Edward L. Bernays in his pioneer work *Crystallizing Public Opinion* (1923), consult a public relations counsel. They ask how to increase their hotel's prestige and so improve their business. In less sophisticated times, the answer might have been to hire a new chef, to improve the plumbing, to paint the rooms, or to install a crystal chandelier in the lobby. The public relations counsel's technique is more indirect. He proposes that the management stage a celebration of the hotel's thirtieth anniversary. A committee is formed, including a prominent banker, a leading society matron, a well-known lawyer, an influential preacher, and an "event" is planned (say a banquet) to call attention to the distinguished service the hotel has been rendering the community. The celebration is held, photographs are taken, the occasion is widely reported, and the object is accomplished. Once the celebration has been held the celebration itself becomes evidence that the hotel really is a distinguished institution. The occasion actually gives the hotel the prestige to which it is pretending.

We celebrate the church's announcement, but there is no "new chef" hired to assure the basic treaty right to self-government and economic security to the Indian Nations. American public opinion and the question of Indians have always been in the hands of the church, the "do-gooder," the crusaders with a cause. This has brought about a strange mixture of racial hatred and good intentions which are rarely acknowledged. It is true that in the future world of geopolitics, contemporary indigenous peoples who possess huge natural resources will very likely have to contend with even greater modern power establishments like the oil companies and the multinationals, but in the past and for much of the present, the churches of America have been in charge.

Consider the career of Episcopal Bishop William Hobart Hare, which is the focus of the remainder of this discussion.[1] Bishop Hare's seventeen years of missionary work among the Sioux (Lakota/Nakota/Dakota) Indians in what is now the state of South Dakota, though it represents an astonishingly brief period of time in the continuum of history, has had enormous and lasting influence on Lakota/Dakota lifeways. I am not sure that Bishop Hare would be very supportive of the church leaders of the northwest in their apology, yet, there is something reminiscent about it all.

In 1872 at the age of 34 years, William Hobart Hare, a New Jersey native, accepted the position of Episcopal Bishop to the newly created missionary jurisdiction of Niobrara, named after a great river which runs through Nebraska and South Dakota. He left this region a mere seventeen years later, in 1889, the greater portion of his work done, when the "Great Sioux Reservation" was split up, the Dakota Territory was divided and federal legislation passed which, among other deeds, conferred statehood upon North and South Dakota, and the Allotment Act was passed in the U. S. Congress. Sovereign Indian lands were divided and later sold so that statehood could be conferred upon the region.

The Allotment Act, seen by Indians as one of the unavenged crimes of human history and by the Sioux as the reason for the assassination of The Act's major native critic, Hunkpapa Chieftain Sitting Bull, allowed the theft of two-thirds of the treaty-protected land holdings of Indians across the country to be legalized in the view of certain governmental and political establishments. Bishop Hare's influence and the church's influence, in general, on the public legitimization of that act can hardly be underestimated. This was not the first occasion, of course, of the theft of Indian lands. The Sioux had already witnessed the theft of the sacred Black Hills and other resources two decades earlier.

Hare, an easterner by birth, returned to the west only infrequently after statehood was established, an honored guest of the church and the tribes themselves. What was his role, his intent? What was his influence? What was his responsibility? How are his responsibility and intent the same as or different from those of the current church leaders of America? For what must the Christian churches apologize? Who forgives them? Who blesses them? Indians and whites at this moment in history are attempting to find answers to these and other inquiries.

Not everyone is pleased with the northwestern church counselors who wrote and eventually made public the centennial apology after much private agonizing and public debate. Those objecting to the apology are concerned that, among other things, such a document *devalues the dedication of early missionaries and makes it difficult for current missionaries to continue doing their work among the people of the existing tribal nations.* Thus, the question of the role of the church vis-à-vis native populations in this country and the role of particularly significant historical missionaries such as Bishop Hare of the northern plains is still a matter of much ambiguity and controversy. Though the Episcopal Diocese of Olympia and the Northwest signed the document, it is not safe to assume that any ecclesiastical district in any other area would be in agreement; in other words, there is no unanimous agreement in the matter even now.

What there is agreement about, however, is that without the work of Christian missionaries, which began in the West nearly a hundred years prior to statehood, the federal mandate which meant the dispossession of the tribes and the taking of their lands might not have succeeded. At the very least, some historians tell us, if it had not been for early Christian missions in the West, the treaty-making process with the tribes and the subsequent legislation which appropriated hundreds of thousands of acres of Indian-owned lands for white settlement would not have occurred in the "humane" way that it did. Many historians suggest that land theft of the sort that occurred in America even after the peace treaties were signed was often a more or less bloodless crime and in some way an inevitable function of history. There was, unfortunately, this history says, a massacre of Indians here and there but only in legitimate response to heathen-inspired events. Treaties were made, and if they weren't exactly kept sacred, well, that was only a matter of the need for "progress" and "civilization." The recent public apology brings up the possibility that such a view of history is at the very least untenable.

It is true that the role of the church in the writing of the Constitution and the passage of subsequent federal legislation which authorized statehood for the lands to which tribes held aboriginal title and had inhabited since time immemorial is complicated and blurred not only by the passage of time but also by the collaboration between the church and its flock, both Indian and non-Indian. However, one way to gain insight into the process of history and to understand the initiation and consequence of the recent rare apology by the church is to look closely at the ideas and schemes of church leaders of the past and try to say what connects their histories to the present perception of the role of today's church men and women.

Bishop William Hobart Hare, born to New England sons and daughters of Puritans and Pennsylvania Friends in 1838, is an important collaborating visionary, archetypal as a celebrated paragon of Christian probity both during his tenure in the Dakota Territory and in his life after he left his work with Indians. He still enjoys a remarkable reputation in history as a virtuous, compassionate man of faith.

Yet he was a man who imagined the Indians of his flock as "a solid foreign mass indigestible by our common civilization," and he set in motion the now despised (though still extant) mission school system, urged the establishment of a white occupational military police force on sovereign Indian lands, worked actively for the abrogation of the Sioux Treaty of 1868 as the "moral" solution to the imminent U. S. military invasion of the Black Hills in 1875, defended the "good" men of the corrupt Indian Agency system, and, most important, condemned the presence of Indian reservations as homelands the tribes. "All reservations," he said, "are only necessary evils, temporary expedients." What this meant in

Hare's time, and has meant since, is that Indians are always under strong pressure to deny their privileged sites of native origin and give them up for some supposed moral imperative. The tribal nations' reconstitution of themselves in the modern world as sovereign entities has been made into an ideological contest based on a morality which silences them. The truth is that this man of God had as a goal for the United States the total extinguishment of Indian land title and ownership. This was not an uncommon goal in the nineteenth century, to be sure, but it was hardly appropriate as the focus of a man who called himself "the Indian Advocate." One of the last statements on Indian affairs he made after the turn of century is filled with irony and perhaps described his successors more explicitly than he ever imagined: "There is a certain obtuseness in our Anglo-Saxon stock," he said, "that makes us fail to feel the situation. There is a proud unwillingness to put ourselves in the other man's place, and see with his eyes, yea, a haughty denial that any sentiment can be sacred unless it be our sentiment; that anything can be a real conviction and have any power with another unless it be our conviction."

In light of this history, the question for contemporary scholars and writers concerned with public apologia is the question of how white and Christian America has changed its view toward Indians. What evidence is there that the idea of the extinguishment of Indian land and resource title has been abandoned by modern America? Have the church men and women gone to the U. S. Congress to demand the return of the Black Hills to their rightful owners? Have they looked critically at the white men who, in the name of the American public, sit on the Senate Select Committee on Indian Affairs in Washington, D. C., representing anti-Indian interests in their legislative duties? Is the Public Declaration of Apology to Indians evidence of an important change in attitude toward sovereignty and human rights, or is it just a pledge of support like the recitation of allegiance to the flag, something ephemeral and harmless? Can native tribal people believe that the Christian church no longer works hand-in-glove with other entities to rid itself of what it sees as its Indian work toward progress and civilization?

When clergyman Hare first came into the West in 1861 from the affluent church in Pennsylvania where he was rector, he visited Michigan and Minnesota for about six months, seeking a new climate for his ailing wife. This was his first glimpse of the West and of Indians. He saw that Christian missions were already in progress and made two important observations which reflected the ambiguity of his own thought, and which mirror, even today, the combination of good intentions and racial/cultural hatred which continues to plague all Indian-White relationships.

First, he observed that the extermination of the Sioux by the federal government through such policies as paying a $200 bounty to private individuals to kill Indians who were not willing to live on reserved places and in the appropriate manner, was unconscionable since they were, after all, "humans," but, that their *extermination as Indians* through coercive assimilation was a viable plan. Second, he noted that, in general, Indians were pitiful, wandering, heathen, and savage, and had not been taught "what was good," an observation which was ironically part of the very rationale the federal government used in initiating its extermination policies in the first place. What is important to contemporary native scholars in these observations, is that they provide important historical evidence that the long-denied idea of extermination was, indeed, an actual and pervasive part of the dialogue concerning the "Indian question" during this period.

Much of this dialogue was taking place prior to and during the 1862 uprising of the Eastern Sioux, when Bishop Hare observed the cruelty of Americans and the American government toward Indians who were said to be responsible for the indiscriminate and unprovoked killing of thousands of white settlers. His justification for the cruelty, though it troubled him, was laced with typical Christian rationale: "God meant," he said publicly in the letters he wrote at the time, "that white man's cruelty should turn out for the Indian's eternal good. To flee their misery they flee to Christ." The fact that thousands of them were dying in the process was not viewed as merciless persecution, but as something which could be simply aggrieved and lamented in the Christian tradition.

The Sioux, as one might expect, had a different interpretation of these events and ideas, for they were sent as prisoners to Fort Snelling in Minnesota, families were destroyed, thirty-eight Indian males were hanged publicly in New Ulm in the largest mass execution in the history of the United States—an event authorized by President Abraham Lincoln, who was at the same time said to be freeing black people from slavery— and it was said that the Sioux should leave their homelands, now called the state of Minnesota, forever. More significant, perhaps, is that they were from that time on vilified in contemporary history as barbarous and bloodthirsty.

Bishop Hare had not spent even six months on the plains before he determined and wrote in his letters that the extermination of native culture was a must. Though these were early sentiments, expressed over and over during his brief six months of actual living in the upper plains, they never changed throughout the next two decades as he wandered from one band to the next, going from reservation to reservation establishing churches and baptizing those who chose to collaborate. When he died in 1909, he claimed that ten thousand Sioux were members of the Episcopal church. It did not occur to him that this paltry number of converts was an obscene goal when compared to the thousands who died in the struggle to defend themselves against the increasing strength and power of the peoples and governments who formed and developed America. Is it this kind of "success," then, which causes the guilt that now brings about the apology and request for forgiveness?

Bishop Hare, as representative of the Christian purpose in America, had several abiding interests and goals:

1. To defend the church of England, the Episcopal faith in America, and its colonizing goals, diminishing other religious influences and mapping out the fields of development for the church.

2. To educate the people of Indian country to become "neat, orderly, and to increase their intelligence," a focus firmly based in the notion of white, European racial and cultural superiority.

3. To dedicate his work to the "common good."

4. To make it plain to all that the United States meant to assure that "every soul within its domain shall obey its will."

Hare wrote often of these goals to the church leadership in the East, to his relatives there, and to government officials. Were these goals worthy of Christian thought? If so, why apologize for them? If not, what can be done about the consequences? Or are these still, as I suspect, the goals of the collaboration between church and state in America, the actual truth?

That these goals focused upon the ultimate dispossession of Sioux rights and lands is, in my view, unequivocal. The explicit theft of lands and illegal settlement on sovereign lands speaks for itself, since American Indians were not at that time citizens of the United States, nor were they simply sociological factions to be subsumed through whatever colonial adventures could be thought up and put in place as policy. The time for apologia is long past, and the need for actual political actions on the part of Christian citizens of America in whom the power rests is urgent.

The Coercive Nature of the Church in Indian Life

With almost fanatical discipline and rigid doctrine, the early Christian churches of America defended their dogma, their origins, and their histories. Rarely was there a true sectarian view, and certainly in the work of the early Episcopal church of America and in the mind of

Bishop Hare there was very little room for diversity, small tolerance for differences of interpretation even in the Christian faiths, to say nothing of non-Christian spiritual thought.

When Bishop Hare visited the Mormons in Utah, for example, as an appointee to the Board of Missions of the Episcopal Church in 1871, he called the Mormon religion "gross" and "disgusting." Though he commended the Mormons for "converting the desert into a garden" (an article of faith which even today allows American Christians to take sides with the Jews and against the Arabs in the so-called Palestinian question) he still labeled their religion "a foul blot." He gave little support to the missionaries of other religious schools, a typical stance of early Christian separatism. Red Jacket of the Senecas observed much earlier that this was a trait previously unknown to Indians which caused them to fight with each other about religion after the Christians came into their midst.

As far as his regard for native religious tradition was concerned, Hare dismissed Indian medicine men as "jugglers" and said "their religion is all a cheat." He had no notion of religious freedom for American Indians because he believed them incapable of religious and philosophical thought. The direct infringement and quick prohibition of any form of traditional native religious practice was urged by Bishop Hare in every public utterance on Indian affairs, and he saw no conflict between his claimed role as "Indian advocate" and the complete destruction of the Indian religious view. He called the legitimate Lakota religious movement of the 1890s "a Ghost Dance" and a "delusion of the mind," agreeing with white historians who have also defined it in those terms, which provide a supportive rationale for simple military slaughter of Indians. Hare said that "leaders in the movement have invigorated old heathen ideas with snatches of Christian truth and have managed to excite an amount of enthusiasm which is amazing," and that the movement was "the effort of heathenism grown desperate to restore its vigor and reinstate itself."

By the time the Wounded Knee massacre occurred in 1890, Bishop Hare had left Indian Country and was living in the East, and he blamed Indians for their own deaths. When he wrote of the massacre, he repeated Col. Forsythe's claim that Big Foot's Band of Minneconjou were "off the reserve" and "apparently bent on mischief." Col. Forsythe was then commanding a regiment reorganized after Custer's death, known in history as "Custer's former regiment," and used this assessment in defense of military action clearly gone wrong. Nowhere in the bishop's letters or speeches does he refer to the fact that Big Foot was dying of pneumonia when he was killed by these troops, nor that he was traveling through his own country under a white flag of truce. Nor does he speculate very insightfully about whether or not the killing of over three hundred innocent women and children was worthy of this nation's purpose or recognizable as a Christian ideal. Rather, Bishop Hare's documentation of one of the worst actions this country has ever taken against a helpless people was described as an event that occurred when Forsythe "tried to disarm the Indians who fell upon the troops with savage fury."

Dee Brown in 1970 tried to set the record straight when he published the book *Bury My Heart at Wounded Knee*. Unfortunately, that book concludes as many histories do, with the finality of things and the assumption of death to native nationhood, quoting Black Elk, or should we say John Niehardt, thus: "I did not know then how much was ended. There is no center any longer and the sacred tree is dead." The reality is that American Indian nations all over this continent have survived, they continue to believe in their own survival, and the fundamental assumptions that Indians have fought continuously to establish as the basis for Federal Indian Law affirm that they continue to be sovereign peoples.

Bishop Hare's version of what happened at Wounded Knee was repeated everywhere, and since it was his Episcopal Mission at Pine Ridge which was opened to receive the wounded and dying, his view has largely prevailed in history. Even after seeing the dreadful death scene, though, he continued to counsel according to his policy: "Fight them, feed them, and lead them to self-support," which, of course, meant assimilation and land confiscation.

Give Them Christian Education

There may have been no more powerful destructive force directed toward American Indian life than the narrow-minded, propagandistic educational policies of the Christian missionaries of the nineteenth century (and much of the twentieth). Church folk of the day did not investigate the cultural and political views of the Indians with whom they lived, and if they were confronted with them they simply dismissed them as primitive and irrelevant. They had no understanding of Indian history—who these tribes were and how they lived on this continent and with one another for thousands of years. With regard to the Black Hills and the discovery of gold in 1875, Hare wrote to his sister, "The Indians' attachment to it [the Black Hills] is a passion. This district is the kernel of their nut, yelk [*sic*] of their egg." He was, of course, right about that but did not support it as a legitimate view of the world. The Sioux today, after sixty years of mostly disappointing litigation in the state and federal courts, still say, "Read our lips! The Black Hills are not for sale!" Failing to understand the religious commitment of the Sioux to the land, Hare suggested over and over again during these years that the purchase of the Black Hills would be feasible. "Steps should be taken," he repeated, "to secure a surrender of the tract in question on equitable terms." In 1980 the Supreme Court declared the "taking" of the Black Hills a "theft" and offered the Sioux hundreds of thousands of dollars to rectify the crime. The Sioux Nation at that time filed an injunction to prevent the paying out of this money and has refused any negotiations that did not include the return of lands and land reform as settlement.

In spite of his stubborn failure to understand the Indian perspective of the world, Bishop Hare imagined himself as a pioneer in Indian education. He wrote in 1873, "The sum of the whole matter is this: the Indians are men. We differ from them in degree not in kind. Exactly where, or nearly where, they are now, we once were; what we are now, they will by God's blessing become. The Indians are all as children and all that is needed is what good schools can give them."

This attitude has prevailed, in large part, in the educational systems across the land. And not only Indians have learned this lesson—the white population of America has learned it, too. Robert F. Berkhofer, a historian of our time, explains this kind of flawed thinking in a useful essay included in his book *The White Man's Indian* which is used in many university courses dealing with what is now called "the new historicism":

European thinkers, impressed with their own accomplishments since the Renaissance, argued the idea of progress first in terms of the power of reason. If human nature was the same during all time, then the contribution of the moderns to learning and science appeared as great as that of the ancients; and indeed the achievements of Galileo, Newton, and others seemed to confirm this conclusion. Thanks to the passage of time, history favored the progress of the moderns over previous peoples because society accumulated knowledge over its life cycle. Basic man was what he had always been, but each generation stood on the shoulders of its predecessors in learning.

This theoretical or conjectural history of the Enlightenment developed from four bodies of comparison: (1) between Europeans of modern times and the people of earlier times, (2) between modern Europeans and contemporaneous uncivilized societies, (3) between people of earlier times and modern uncivilized peoples, and (4) comparisons among the observable modern uncivilized themselves. Insofar as these methods were applied to the American Indian, it could be assumed that the early condition of present civilized societies and the present conditions of primitive peoples were enough alike as to suggest commonality in origin, dismissing culture and racial experiences as possible motivators.

"The history produced by these rules may not have been accurate," concluded Berkhofer, "but no matter as long as it provided a plausible beginning point in time for the analysis of the history of human institutions. In this sense, the best history was not real history but an ideal or theoretical history that pointed out the normal, (i.e., natural) development of humankind's behavior in contradistinction to what really happened. These rules and this goal made possible the many studies of the origins of social inequality, of the state, of the economy, of religion, and of other institutions produced by the philosophers."

Armed with the kind of historical perspective spoken of here by Berkhofer, Bishop Hare accepted the stereotypes of Indian childlikeness, Indian savagery, and Indian inferiority. Concentrating on educating the Indian by taking him at an early age away from his home and his likewise savage, childlike parents, he misunderstood the nature of learning in the native societies to which he ministered. He dismissed the inherent conflict in this educational process: that his method of acting as an agent of change was hostile to the Sioux notion that their children would develop better if left to themselves.

"God pity the poor Indians in their teepees," he wrote to his associates, and he directed the Sioux children to chop more wood for their drafty schoolrooms. In many cases, these were the sons and daughters of the chieftains of the Sioux Nation, taught from infancy that the white man's way of life was dishonorable.

"How much better it is", said the Bishop at Thanksgiving time in 1877, one year after Custer's defeat at the Little Big Horn, "to give them Christian education than to let them grow up wild to entrap and massacre our soldiers, as my current students' fellow-countrymen did with Custer's gallant troops."

To the end, he did not understand the nature of the conflict between the invading white man and the people who claimed indigenousness in the upper plains. Within four years, Sitting Bull would be shot to death by the colonial police force which was by now, with Hare's urging, stationed on every reservation in the Dakotas, and the resistance leader's children would be forced to submit to the Bible and the plow against their wills. Bishop Hare took great pride in capturing these celebrated youngsters for the church.

The Christian educational impulse was not, of course, Bishop Hare's lone invention. It was present in the federal government and the Indian nations when they made several early treaties dealing with Indian education, among them the following:

1. The treaty of July 23, 1851, with the Sioux (10 *Stat.* 949)

2. The treaty of August 5, 1851, with the Sioux (1110 *Stat.* 954)

3. The treaty of April 19,1858, with the Yankton Sioux (11 *Stat.* 743)

4. The treaty of June 19, 1858, with the Sioux bands (12 *Stat.* 1031)

5. The treaty of October 14, 1865, with the Lower Brule Sioux (14 *Stat.* 699)

6. The treaty of April 29, et seq., 1869, with the Sioux Nation (15 *Stat.* 635) and many others.

Churches were awarded thousands of acres of Indian land by the U.S. Congress during these treaty negotiations, and it was certainly the responsibility of Bishop Hare and others like him to give structure and substance to the institutions which would carry out the treaty stipulations. Unfortunately, no real Indian model of education arose from this attempt. Because of the tenacity of Bishop Hare's righteousness, and his inability to shake off his long-standing belief in his own superiority, the unfortunate Sioux were enmeshed in a very coercive and some say damaging educational system before they knew what had happened to them.

Hare acknowledged two particular problems which he stated early in his writings to his colleagues. First, he said, the Indians he had to deal with were the most "reckless and wild" of all humankind, and the country was incredibly desolate. Secondly, he said, "emissaries of evil had reached the Indians long before the Cross," thus making his chores that much more difficult.

There were only four possibilities for the future of Indians in this country and in this educational system, according to Bishop Hare: (1) if Indians were meant to be slaves, "hewers of wood and drawers of water," then, the Bishop said, it was the church's responsibility to fit them for their lot in life; (2) if they were meant to merge into "our own race," this meant intermarriage, and it was the church's responsibility, the Bishop contended, to "make them fit for intermarriage with us"; (3) if they were to die out, it was the church's duty to prepare them for their departure; and (4) if they were to be physically exterminated, he and the church would have no part of it.

Thus, the early emissaries of the Christian church conceived of the inhabitants of the New World, people who had developed their cultures over thousands of years, only in terms of slavery and genocide. Such thinking did not occur in ancient and medieval times; rather, it occurred in the middle of the nineteenth century, when the Brooklyn Bridge was being built, Wesleyan College for women was being established in Georgia, the Republican Party was being organized, and the fifteenth amendment guaranteeing blacks the right to vote became a part of the Constitution.

The contradiction between the ideals of Christianity and the reality lived and remembered by the millions of Indians on this continent, including the members of my family, is disheartening to say the least. That Indian lands, and rights, and peoples were presided over by such representatives of humanity demonstrates for the world to see that Indians have little to be forgiving about and even less for which to be grateful.

The Christian Commitment to the "Common Good" Takes Precedence

After the establishment of Bishop Hare's schools for the education of the Sioux—St. Paul's at Yankton, St. John's at Cheyenne River, St. Mary's at Rosebud, and St. Elizabeth's at Standing Rock—the bishop wrote a constant stream of letters trying to get rid of what was then and is now called the reservation system. Ignoring the fact that Indian reservations were now Indian homelands, protected under treaty and holding special status as "nations-within-a-nation," he railed for the "common good." He had at this later time extended his administration to whites, not just Indians, and said, "from the beginning I struggled against the notion that we were missionaries to Indians alone and not missionaries to all men." Acting as though there was no antagonism, Indian lands were not being stolen every day, and Indian children were not failing in the educational systems to which they were subject, Hare adopted the stance that the work of the church was plausible, humane, and liberal. This blinded stance ignored the need for a true critique of how Americans were behaving toward the indigenes.

In 1884, Bishop Hare started All Saints School for Girls in one of the largest urban centers, Sioux Falls, South Dakota, for the daughters of his missionaries. Few of the daughters of Indian missionary families were admitted, although the famed Dakota linguist and scholar Ella Deloria was one of the first, long after the Bishop's death. During World War II, when many native soldiers were drafted into the U. S. Army, other Indian girls including myself and my elder sister, Kathryn, were enrolled. My sister and I stayed there for one year and then were not accepted for the second or subsequent years, though our parents were not given any reasons for the refusal to readmit us. Our assumption was that we simply didn't measure up. Mostly, the school's enrollment was made up of the daughters of wealthy and important contributors to the church. At the close of his tenure, Bishop Hare lived on the campus of All Saints School for short periods of time. He traveled to the east and went abroad while he also ministered to small towns that were springing up all over: Madison, Howard, Carthage, Woonsocket, Elk Point, Groton.

In his advancing years, he took great pride in his influence. He often read from his files for church advocates. One of his final reports, the seventeenth annual, was of particular interest to South Dakotans who were now settled on previously designated treaty lands. Bishop Hare in that report called the Congressional Dawes Severalty Act, (Allotment Act) "an achievement of incalculable value." Then he said, "Now, the next step is that the remainder of the country can be sold to white settlers and the two races thus can be intermingled." His focus on the "common good" in defense of the interests of most of the whites in the area made beggars of the men and women of the Sioux Nation. Even today, at the close of the twentieth century, they still suffer the economic consequences of land loss and an underdeveloped economic system very possibly as a direct result of the land policies set forth in the Christianizing years of their early contact with whites—the very policies perpetuated and defended by Christian missionaries.

Every Soul Shall Obey the Will of the Nation

Bishop Hare, like many of his contemporaries, could always find the rationale to defend "the will of the nation"; indeed, it was an all-consuming ideal which permeated much of his work. He depended upon the national spirit to accomplish whatever was out of bounds for the church in the matter of national progress. When he advocated a colonial police force on reservation, (i.e., sovereign) lands, for example, he reasoned, "While the church will not use force, herself, she should countenance its use by proper authorities." He wrote constantly about the recalcitrance of the people at the Red Cloud (Pine Ridge) and Spotted Tail Agencies (Rosebud) in the west, which he saw as notorious for violence. Today, the Oglalas and the Sicangu of those agencies are leaders among the several Sioux tribes in the litigation process for the return of lands stolen from them in the decades prior to the twentieth century. Hare wrote to his contemporaries many times of the "disturbances" on these two reservations.

"There are some who believe that the turbulence of the Indians is owing to the wrongdoing of their agents," he protested, "but these agents had been nominated by the Executive Committee of the Indian Commission of our church and I have reason to believe that they are honorable men and the cause of the trouble should be sought elsewhere." "Just because Indians have been wronged," he said, "they are not always in the right."

He condemned the Oglalas and the Upper Brules, saying, "They are the most distant of the Sioux from civilizing influences and the last who have accepted a position with the government." He went on to say, "Their agencies are the resort during the winter of multitudes of northern Indians (Minneconjous, Sans Arcs, Uncpapas, etc.), the wilder spirits among them find these sojourners congenial company and combined they constitute a turbulent party."

He could tell uplifting stories of the compliance of the Santee Charles A. Eastman with the Christian life (he eventually married the white missionary Miss Elaine Goodale in what they both viewed as an experiment toward assimilation) and Truth Teller, a nephew of a hereditary chief of considerable note at Crow Creek who "handed me his scalplock and war eagle feather and the drum," and declared he would "give up all heathen rites and ceremonies and worship only the God of civilization." But he was hard pressed to find people among the Oglala and Sicangu of like persuasion. The Bishop often considered his life in danger at the hands of these "hostile Indians" who from the outset resisted government efforts to compel them to "scratch the ground"—their description of farming. They believed that agriculture was a skill for the white man to acquire, not suitable for Indian lifeways.

Perhaps the most ambiguous, puzzling, and ultimately callous of Bishop Hare's opinions concerned the Black Hills, sacred lands to the Sioux. While he had insisted that an occupational police force be placed on Sioux lands to force the Sioux into signing treaties, he did not advocate maintaining federal troops on the borders to prevent white intrusion into the treaty-protected Black Hills area. Indeed, he wrote to the president numerous times suggesting that his missionaries would be endangered by any military force that might be in the area outside of reservation boundaries. But he wrote also that verifying the presence of gold in the hills would be useful, thereby condoning the illegal expeditions of countless people, including G. A. Custer. He said that such action, while it would be in violation of the 1868 treaty, should bring about the simple abrogation of the treaty. Thus it would be reasonable for such a military force to move into the area. Bishop Hare admitted that signing treaties with Indians and abrogating them was not always as ethical as he cared for, but, under pressure, it could be construed as "for the common good."

Bishop Hare constantly sought reasons to defend the authority of the federal government, and eventually President Ulysses S. Grant did what was asked of him. He removed the troops who guarded the treaty boundaries, and the Black Hills were taken by thieves.

While the Bishop had wanted a public document abrogating the treaty, he nonetheless accepted the "opening" of the Black Hills saying, finally, "I foresaw that no power on earth could shut out our white people from that country if it really contained valuable deposits of gold and other mineral." For some of the same reasons that he had spent almost twenty years in working toward the destruction of Sioux culture and religion, he stated in his official documents that it might be worthwhile to protect lumber and agricultural resources for Indian use, but the gold discovery made the Black Hills automatically "for sale for a fair equivalent" to the white man. In spite of his notion that the United States had *"a sacred obligation of a great to a weak people,"* he sanctioned the theft of the gold from the Black Hills which, in practical terms, meant the theft of the land itself.

Some white scholars and writers objected to the policy advocated by the church. One of them was Helen Hunt Jackson, very nearly a contemporary of the Bishop's, who provides further explanation of the views held by supporters of Hare's position in a book called *A Century of Dishonor* (1881). She investigated the reports of the commissioners who dealt with the Traverse de Sioux (eastern bands) during earlier negotiations and discovered that annuities were not paid to the Indians because "the well ascertained fact (is) that no greater curse can be inflicted on a tribe so little civilized as the Sioux than to have large sums of money coming to them as annuities."

Jackson reported that the commissioner said, "as a matter of humanity and duty toward this helpless race, [we should] make every exertion in our power not to place much money at their discretion." The government then proposed to pay for Mississippi Valley lands in Minnesota at only two and a half cents per acre. "This is not selfishness at all", seethed reformer Jackson, "it is the purest of philanthropy!!"

Economic self-sufficiency was for whites, according to this thinking, which the commissioners and the bishop seemed to share, but not for Indians, who must be kept poverty-stricken and in a state of beggary as a function of Christian charity!

Recently in the northern plains there has been some cursory talk of "reconciliation," a declaration of it having been made by a former governor of South Dakota, but there has been no dialogue on the return of stolen lands. Today, Indians in this region (and many others) remain the poorest of all racial and cultural groups in the United States. They suffer health and education problems in far greater numbers than most Americans. In the region, Bishop Hare's churches and schools still "serve" the Sioux, but they rarely comment publicly or aggregately on the litigation by the tribes for the return of certain portions of the Black Hills for the purpose of economic survival and self-sufficiency and religious life. They are silent on the taking of Indian lands along the Missouri River for hydropower. They do not object when the States Attorney General sues the tribes capriciously on issues of jurisdiction.

Some may say that there is great sympathy for the dreadful situation in which Indians find themselves politically and economically. Certainly that is true of many churchgoing people in the region, but they have developed *no active intellectual position* beyond the pledges of support illustrated at the beginning of this essay. To develop such a position would take real, coherent, harsh, and truthful self-criticism of the role of Christian churches in public Indian policy.

Part Three

WHO WILL TELL
THE STORIES?

7

The Relationship of a Writer to the Past

Art, a Literary Principle, and the Need to Narrate

In 1862 the United States Government, at the order of Abraham Lincoln, who in the same week signed the Emancipation Proclamation, hanged thirty-eight Dakota Sioux patriots in a public execution in Minnesota, calling them criminals. The event is notable, in a nativist's view, not because it is the largest mass execution in the history of America, but because the Dakotah grandmothers and those who were to become the grandmothers witnessed it. It was forever etched in their minds and it became one of the private horrors of colonialism. One of my grandmothers, Eliza Grey Cloud Renville (1857–1947), when she spoke of it at all, spoke in the tribal language of her childhood, and she called it a crime against humanity. A child witness to death, she knew all the stories, and she told her grandchildren as many as she could bear.

For those who remain, the telling of such a mass execution may be seen now as the beginning of a literary and historical narration about Indians and whites which has been directed as much by tragic songs as by the force of arms or the drama of politics. In midwestern history this event and the events which led up to war are often described as "the Dakota Conflict," a sad and inevitable Gunga Din and Khyber Rifle kind of story told by those who took over the land. Whites have told the story, which has gone from hatred to adoration, from vilification to romanticization, from abuse to respect, and back again. Indians have been content to turn their thoughts backward in time. In either case, the writer has now come to a terrible understanding that the story is in a state of chaos.

An examination of the dichotomy between the stories that Indian America tells and the stories that White America tells is crucial to the current literary criticism wars. And who gets to tell the stories is a major issue of our time.

The practitioners of American letters, along with the nation builders who accompanied them, have failed to take into account the inconvenient reality that Indian America has always had its own quiet word(s) and language(s) which it has used and composed and clung to in an attempt to assert its own distinction in the age of empire. This quiet voice, tribal by nature, is at the core of all that is wrong yet all that is right about America's literature and art; its absence has been a failure to accept the whole phenomenon of humanity, and its belated acceptance tells us we cannot any longer as artists accept our own supposedly benign inadequacies.

Partly because of the survival of that unexpected distinction, which has been so much in opposition to the imperial legacy of those who took over the land, contemporary America has been forced into a furious debate about what should and should not be taught in its schools, what should and should not be published and made into art, what it means to claim the power to narrate, and how crucial it is to block dissenting narratives from audience.

The strong literary argument in defense of the narrative voice of the nineteenth- and twentieth-century Euro-American culturists seeks to declare the indigene *persona non grata* and imaginatively dominate the literary landscape. The result has been, until now, an almost unchallenged vision of America's superiority over those whose ancient mythologies of the land, it has been thought, might deform and transfigure the newcomer. There has been little recognition during this century, at least until these waning decades, that the American Indian voice might, on the contrary, stir the human community to a moral view which would encompass all of humanity, not just selected parts of it.

The quiet voice of American Indians, and the intellectual voice of the Sioux Nation in particular, began to be heard at the turn of the century when the Sioux sought to file suit against the federal government for the theft of the Black Hills.[1] This was not just politics. It was a creative process which, like any artful activity, would follow the stress lines of history and validate the mythology which was and is at the heart of the people. The Sioux were among the first of the indigenes to do this creative thing at a time when American Indians who did not have ready access to American court systems were heavily stereotyped by American scholars and writers as "vanishing," "degraded," or "caught between two cultures."

Always vivid in the imagination of the American public, Indians in general have been freely examined by "outsiders"—white scholars and fiction writers. Those who hanged the Dakota men in Minnesota called them savage, bloodthirsty, and cruel. Those who opposed them in the courts called them foolish, inadequate, and trivial. Probably no Indians more than the Sioux have with such regularity and frequency been used and abused by the image makers. Because of this unwelcome attention, it was the Sioux who were first among American Indians to challenge what they saw as a distorted vision of themselves.

The culture of empire has always been reflected in the novel, and novels about Indians are no exception. What is new is that the critique by Indians themselves of such works has in the last two decades become part of the public discourse. There is also the obvious rise of native writers of contemporary fiction since the 1968 Pulitzer Prize for the novel *House Made of Dawn* went to a young Kiowa intellectual named N. Scott Momaday from New Mexico. This novel has become a classic in modern fiction.

Though novels by Indians are, perhaps, an innovation of our time, novels about Indians by white writers have been around for a couple of centuries in this country as well as in Europe. The 1979 publication of the novel *Hanta Yo*, however, written by a white woman, Ruth Beebe Hill of the San Juan Islands in Washington, brought about a defining moment in the native challenge to the fictionalized Indian in America and to the domination of the literary imagination by Euro-America.

In spite of the fact that it was not, *Hanta Yo* was called "an Indian epic" in the April 16, 1979, *Newsweek* book section: "The season's most successful first novelist is a 65-year-old woman who lives on a remote island, Friday Harbor, in the Pacific Northwest," said the reviewer, "and spent 28 years researching and writing her bestseller. Even more remarkable is the book itself. *Hanta Yo* (Doubleday, $14.95) is an unsensational, painstakingly authentic, 834-page saga about American Indians around 1800." The Sioux considered the novel's depiction of their lives and histories false and obscene, and surprisingly, they began to say so publicly—in the media, in academia, and everywhere in between.

In South Dakota, the tribal homelands, the Black Hills Claims and Treaties Council passed a unanimous resolution condemning the book and denying the council's participation in the preparation of the proposed television miniseries. The Sicangu Sioux through the Lakota

Studies department of Sinte Gleska College, located on the Rosebud
Sioux Reservation and then less than a decade old, prepared a manuscript articulating the novel's inauthenticity and errors.[2] Native scholars
such as Professor of Lakota Studies at Sinte Gleska, Victor Douville,
Smithsonian anthropologist and member of the Standing Rock Sioux
Tribe, Dr. Joallyn Archambaulte, and historian Vine Deloria, also a
member of the Sioux tribes, were adamant in their condemnation of
the book as historical fiction. Most offensive to the Lakota people were
depictions of sodomy, oral sex, and a mother's eating of her newborn's
afterbirth as ritual religious acts. While such acts might occur in any
culture and historical era, said the Indian critics, the author's claim that
these were ritual acts and religious practices inspired by the cultural
belief system of the Sioux was patently false and obscene. The native
scholars went on to describe sexuality in terms of the human spirit, and
the afterbirth material as sacred material which required appropriate
disposal by formal burial rite.

The novel was edited by Lisa Drew at Doubleday, who also edited
Alex Haley's *Roots*. The film and TV rights were immediately sold to
David Wolper, the controversial docu-drama king (who was eventually
enjoined in 1983 and prevented at least for that moment by Elizabeth
Taylor from doing her life story for ABC, for six figures). Paperback
rights went to Warner Books for more than $200,000. After much wran-
gling, a five-hour adaptation of *Hanta Yo*, renamed *Mystic Warrior* was
shown on ABC and, in spite of tribal objections, native consultants
were hired. One of the major consultants was a Lakota newspaper man
from Pine Ridge Reservation in South Dakota, Tim Giago, now editor and publisher of *Indian Country Today*, a flourishing, native-owned
newspaper.

The television production was a miserable recreation of the novel
which satisfied no one and was notable only as a rather strange interlude
fitted uncomfortably between the twelve-hour production of *Roots* and
the ten-hour dramatization of Colleen McCullough's best seller, *The
Thorn Birds*. It is ironic that *Hanta Yo*, the only fictional Indian story being
told during this period of intense activism, was reaching thousands of
uninformed Americans who, if they knew anything at all, knew that the
American Indian Movement had recently "taken over" a tiny hamlet in
South Dakota called Wounded Knee as a revolutionary act protesting
federal Indian policies of the period. Thus, as art, the white woman's
narrative became simply a part of the sensational television fare of genre
fiction exploited as the "authentic Indian *Roots*."

Ruth Beebe Hill, at that time actively promoting her work as historical fiction, scoffed at the criticism from Indians and was quoted in

several area newspapers as saying, "The Indians who are objecting are misled, misguided, or they haven't read my book." Indian critics were dismissed by Mrs. Hill and her Indian "informant," Lorenzo Blacksmith, called Chunksa Yuha for publicity purposes, as "actually, only a half-dozen persons; we call that group *the whining six-pack*." Hill said of contemporary Indian life, "There isn't anything Indian today except people drinking and fighting and fussing and the rest of it and a few of those wonderful old people." She added that she was "getting sick" of charges that *Hanto Yo* was a fraud. "My knowledge is of the archaic language," she said. She continued to claim that her novel was the result of "30 years of painstaking scholarly research and field work." She was a popular speaker at schools and universities across the West, and her book was translated, it was said, into more than a dozen foreign languages.

The people of the Sioux Nation occupy hundreds of thousands of fragile, treaty-protected acres in the northern plains of the United States. They have an oral history which makes them seem unconnected to the history of American ideas and literary evaluations. Their resistances and oppositions, therefore, are little known and even less understood.

The *Hanta Yo* controversy became a watershed event in the emergence of a critical voice for the Sioux, and the American public saw and heard, perhaps for the first time, a tribal model of non-European thought concerning self-definition in a colonial world of art and history. Thus this literary event became an important tribal landmark.

A scholarly journal, the *Indian Historian*, had emerged during the activist decade of the sixties in San Francisco, California, as a primary native voice in academia. Founded and published by Rupert Costo and Jeannette Henry, it was one of the first notable scholarly journals to publish important tribal critiques about *Hanta Yo*. A major commentary, written by Dr. Beatrice Medicine, a native anthropologist and Dakota Sioux scholar from Wakpala, SD, appeared in the summer of 1979. She wrote as follows:

Native people living in the contemporary world are usually the last to know and have something to say about what is being published concerning us.

This is true whether the work is in history, anthropology, psychology, education, or fiction. Recently, much social science research or grant applications have emphasized that the projected research is a result of "tribal council approval." In many cases, these councils do not inform the poor and powerless people in the hinterlands of the reservations, who are the captive objects of such studies.

This unawareness appears to be true in the advent of the book *Hanta Yo* by Ruth Beebe Hill. Hill had the linguistic aid of a Mdewakantowan Dakota who calls himself Chunksa Yuha. In my view, the two combine to make a "dreaming pair," and the book is evidence of this.

First I shall detail my involvement prior to the actual reading of the book. I had heard of the book while listening to a radio program in which one Lisa Drew was addressing an audience. I wrote Ms. Drew at Doubleday to ask which tribe was being touted as The Indian *Roots*. An assistant responded, "It is a two-generation history of a family of Dakota Indians." Obviously, the promotional barrage touting the book as an Indian *Roots* leaned on the reputation of Alex Haley's book *Roots*. To compare this book to Haley's is at least fatuous.

Then, there appeared an article entitled "Ruth Hill Became Indian to Write Epic of the Sioux," by Peggy Thomson in the *Smithsonian* (December, 1978). This article is ample evidence that Native Americans are still at the mercy of journalists, free-lance writers, script writers, and other establishment media forces. The article, however, has given the book a certain authenticity lodged in the bosom of *Smithsonian* magazine as an authority in the field of ethnic studies, a reputation it does not deserve.

But linguists and anthropologists at the Smithsonian Institution were quick to point out that the magazine was not connected in any way with their austere institution. Yet, none of them has produced a contrary review; nor have any of them offered a statement pointing out their disassociation with the magazine. To be charitable, it is probably because either they had attempted to read the book and could not, or they had not taken the trouble to read it at all.

The fashion of advocacy for native peoples is no longer trendy in the social sciences, it would appear. It is seldom evident in the humanities, especially in the academic regions of history.

It is debatable that Mrs. Hill, as she claims, has translated the entire book from archaic Dakota, as she claims to have done. The prose does not present the rich, colorful and humorous, nuances of the Dakota language. Nor does metaphor and philosophy come through. The choppy sing-song effect of the Dakota verbalizations [is] tiresome. Phrases such as Ahbleza, saying, "I say I have enough, enough of enough" (p. 471) is enough to give the impression of the inaccurate linguistics effect. Many utterances of the characters (one has to call them utterances because they certainly are not representative of Dakotah speech), ending with "say so, say so" [are] repetitious and boring.

Finally, Dr. Medicine said,

The idea of *ritualizing* sodomy and homosexuality is inexcusable. Hill's descriptions of sexual acts give credence to the image of a stereotypic, presumed lust-filled rapaciousness of all Indians. The Lakota, next to the Cheyenne, were one of the most sexually restrained native societies which have been documented. There were good reasons for these proscriptions and they must be understood in the totality of the culture. But, anything goes to provide the market with a best seller!

The danger lies in the possibility that future students who are searching for an ethos and world view of the Lakota, and too lazy to do their own research, will rely on this historical novel which is now seen by Ruth Hill as "truth." According to the *Chicago Tribune* (May 17, 1979) " 'Indian definition of truth is what happens,' says Hill. 'And, everything in this book happened.' "

The only reasons that native persons would find this book appealing, Dr. Medicine asserts, are these:

They are too lazy to do their own research.
They have been deprived of access to their oral history.
They grew up as culturally disenfranchised individuals because of the pressures of being "White Dakota."
They have been living outside the group through no fault of their own, having been adopted or fostered.
They were simply ashamed of being Lakota/Dakota.
They do not know the language and culture of the people.

Dr. Medicine later became research director for the Royal Commission on Aboriginal Peoples in Ottawa, Canada. She is the niece of the noted Lakota/Dakota scholar of the 1930s, Ella Deloria, and was an active participant in both the First Convocation of American Indian Scholars (Princeton University) and the Second Convocation of American Indian Scholars (Aspen Institute of Humanistic Studies). She is noted for doing important tribal research among Dakota Indians, documenting the urbanization of Indians in Detroit, Chicago, and Los Angeles, and teaching the first course on the role of women in Native American societies at Dartmouth University.

Another native scholar and activist, Lois Red Elk, representing members of the Sioux Alliance in Los Angeles, California, and members of seven Sioux reservation tribal councils also spoke of their responses to the book. They appeared as protesters at the university campuses where Hill was scheduled to speak. On one such occasion, Lakota historian Ben Black Bear, Sr., addressed a university audience on the University of Nebraska campus in Lincoln, saying in the Lakota language, "I wouldn't look upon the Indian people as behaving like *pte* (buffalo), as she has done. We are humans."

Stanley Red Bird, President of the Medicine Men and Associates, Inc., of South Dakota, along with Francis Whitebird, vice president, Iver Crow Eagle, Sr., secretary, Narcisse Eagle Bear, treasurer, and Ted Thin Elk, sergeant-at-arms, along with twenty-three associates, signed a white paper which condemned the book, stating that it is "inaccurate and presents a completely erroneous picture of the culture and social life of the Sioux." They said the book "was a total embarrassment to the people of the Rosebud. *Wowapi ki le un Wasicu Wiyan ki le Sicangu Lakota ki ihankeya wo'istelya unkekin' an pelo. Wowapi ki le Ihangyuapi wasteke lo.*"

Hill was at that time translating the book's title as "clear the way," arguing that it is both a war cry and a metaphysical statement of Lakota/Dakota spiritualism. Among the contemporary Sioux who speak the language every day and know the etymology of words, *hanta yo* is simply a throwaway phrase for dismissing an irritating child, equivalent to the English "scram" or "move."

A more serious objection to the linguistic issues brought up by Hill's novel is that the author overstated Sioux individualism, extolling what Lakota scholars called "the language of ego" and depicting the Lakota as free from all restraint. Hill, a friend and ardent admirer of the radical individualist Ayn Rand, was accused of inappropriately projecting Rand's notions onto the Sioux, a communal people constrained by the rules of the *tiospaye*, a cultural and spiritual construct based upon familial blood ties.

Chunksa Yuha, Hill's informant, initially told the news media that he was "kept out of schools and away from white contact until the age of twelve" to learn the ancient suppressed ceremonies which Hill and he described in the novel. Later he was unmasked as Lorenzo Blacksmith, the son of an Episcopal deacon, who was listed in the National Archives of the Bureau of Indian Affairs as a student of BIA schools between the ages of five and eighteen.

In the interview with the *Smithsonian Magazine*, Hill said that she grew up in Cleveland Heights, Ohio, and became friends with scientists, authors, and film directors. There is no reason to doubt these biographical details. She said she intended the book to undo the damage of early missionaries and explorers and the damage of Hollywood "where actors mouth 24 Indian words." "Nobody else," she claimed, "ever told the story from the inside, using the ancient Sioux language to develop the Indians' point of view. Caucasian and Indian are diametrically opposed. There had to be just what there was . . . Chunksa Yuha and Ruth Hill diametrically opposed and remote." In the final paragraphs of the interview, a description of the informant's singing and spirituality is described as follows, and the relationship between the author and her Indian becomes clearer, not so diametrically opposed after all:

The Indian sings in the five-note minor tone the hunka song which begins like a wind with its aspirated sounds . . . the song of the hide-and-seek for the tepee of the relative-by-choice. He sings the theme of the book, explaining that it will not accompany a war party bursting over the rim of a hill yelling, but, rather, one man on horseback. It is the song of a lone warrior, singing to raise his full power, horse and rider taking on the power of the song as their own. "Hanta yo! Clear the Way! In a sacred manner I come." Commanding the life force: "Grandfather, hear me! Every creature that ever flew, walked, crawled. . . . I own the earth and so I come."

"That's all the Indian religion there ever was," says Mrs. Hill. "No God, gods, Great Mystery, but a command to the life force. If you're not Indian it takes 30 years to discover it."

As for herself: "I don't to this day wear moccasins. No way! I've never been given a name or made 'an honorary princess.' It's no compliment. I've never been adopted by an Indian tribe."

She goes livid over activist Indian movements led by "Indians with makeup from the Avon lady. Do I feel guilty about the land? Hell, no. I do not."

The relationship that every writer (and critic) has to his own past which, in the Hill case, reduces itself to the dominant Europeanism so prevalent in literary studies in America and so pervasive in every Indian fiction in America, can only be called political. Edward W. Said, the Palestinian critic, has perhaps quite unintentionally legitimized the political objection of Native American critics to inaccurate imaginings, though he doesn't even mention the tribal model(s) of criticism and may be quite unaware of them. In *Culture and Imperialism* (1993), he states unequivocally that narrative often "has a structure of attitude and reference that entitles the European authorial subject to hold on to an overseas territory, derive benefits from it, depend on it, but ultimately refuse it autonomy or independence." He could just as well have said "a domestic nation" and used the experience of America's First Nation in his discourse. The Sioux politician/lawyer/scholar, Vine Deloria, Jr., though not a literary critic by his own admission, was decades ahead of Said, of course, as far as Indian readers have been concerned.

This relationship to the past is individualistic as often as it is communal, and it is sometimes ephemeral and, certainly, unclarified in the critical work now available because of its antagonism to the politicization of scholarship. Nevertheless, it is useful in accounting for views that are not tribally specific, such as that of the Kiowa intellectual, N. Scott Momaday, who has never been accused of defensive nationalism.

Momaday's important review of *Hanta Yo* appeared in the *Washington Post* at the time of this controversy:

Someone has said that, for Americans, history is by and large a contemporary invention. It serves to show us where we are on the map of time, but our frame of reference is very narrow. Our recent celebration of the nation's bicentennial reminded us that our whole history as a nation extends only from here to there. On the far side of 1776 there is little that is sharply defined; there is darkness reaching to creation.

Hanta Yo . . . which means "clear the way" . . . is a novel set in that vague distance, about a people whose history is essentially invisible. It is the story of a band of Indians who lived on this continent 200 years ago, before the coming of the white man to their homeland in the northern Great Plains.

It is a large novel . . . and, in some ways a novel of large pretensions. The dust jacket has it that *Hanto Yo* is a major achievement in the exploration of American Indian culture. It may be so, but it is difficult to tell what that achievement is, exactly.

Part of the difficulty arises with the further claim that the book is "a linguistic tour de force." It is said to have been translated from present day English into an old Dakotah/Lakotah dialect and then retranslated into an English based upon the 1806 edition of Webster's Dictionary.

These maneuvers, surely very complicated, are supposed to result in a faithful reflection of the Indian idiom. But, such a claim seems gratuitous. I suspect that one does not reproduce the language of the Indians by reverting to the English of 1806. And, yet, the author, as well as her publisher, seems concerned to make such an argument.

In a note to the reader, Ruth Beebe Hill writes: "Admit, assume, because, believe, could, doubt, end, expect, faith, forget, forgive, guilt, how, if, mercy, pest, promise, should, sorry, storm, them, us, waste, we, weed . . . neither these words nor the conceptions for which they stand appear in this book; they are the white man's import to the New World, the newcomer's contribution to the vocabulary of the man he called Indian. Truly, the parent Indian families possessed neither these terms nor their equivalents."

It is hard to take this statement seriously. In order to do so, one must necessarily formulate the impression that Indian languages are extremely impoverished. But, of course they are not. To the extent that one can generalize (there are at least a hundred living Indian languages today), they are rich, intricate, highly developed. [Ed. note: Most linguists suggest that there are over 300 such languages today.]

But I am done, now, with quibbling. All of this makes very little difference, as far as I can see, in the verbal texture of the book, which, though brittle at some points, is not tedious and never seems archaic. The reader is not, I think, moved to question whether or not the language is a true reflection of the Indian idiom. And this is as it should be, after all. The story should, and does, appeal to him on his own terms on the basis of his own experience, linguistic and otherwise.

Hanta Yo, 25 years in the making, is a substantial novel, impressive in both conception and execution. In the course of the long, many-faceted narrative, there is revealed a fascinating world. In one sense it is a small, nearly private world, a world so exclusive as to be available only in the pages of the book. But, it is a whole world, too, full of good things and bad.

Curiously, characterization is at best a secondary quality of this novel. Numerous figures come into view, make their mark and recede into the current of time. None succeeds to the isolation of heroism. But as happens, this is somehow appropriate. For the heroism of *Hanta Yo* consists not in the individual but in the group, the Mahto band of the Teton Sioux.

What we see, and what works a wonder again and again in our souls, is the humanity that informs this special world. It is noble and real and pervasive.

Much could be made of this assessment from the point of view of a tribal critic interested in monitoring the book's fraudulent claim to fictional classicism, a "classic" being a work that stems from literary tradition (i.e., the "Indian *Roots*"). I was, frankly, puzzled when I read the review. Momaday seems to be headed in one direction in this review but veers in another at the end with what might be described as insipid clichés about tribal wisdom.

Surely, one of the important observations about such an articulation in the review is that it seems to emerge from a built-in chauvinism or romanticism concerning Indian self-identity—not tribally specific Lakota, or Hopi, or Navajo identity, for example; rather "Indian" self-identity, which is often external and "Ameri-centric." That imagined special world of the Indian beckons the nontribal reader, the cultural outsider. Ceremonies of belonging don't necessarily require cultural or tribal-specific accuracy for some readers and critics, especially those removed from the vital cultural presence of a specific group. Thus, Dr. Medicine's cultural explanation of why some native persons might be inclined to say good things about the book transcends the literary assessment articulated with such clarity by Momaday. The fiction of Hill's novel concerning a "noble" world has its appeal.

Other writers who write from the perspective of a colonized people have commented upon such paradoxes of thought, most significantly the African poet, Wole Soyinka, who said in *Myth, Literature, and the African World*,

Negritude trapped itself in what was primarily a defensive role, even though its accents were strident, its syntax hyperbolic and its strategy aggressive . . . negritude stayed within a pre-set system of Eurocentric intellectual analysis of both man and his society, and tried to re-define the African and his society in those externalized terms.

What Soyinka has said has happened to negritude has also happened to "Indian-ness," in many instances. The "pre-set system of Eurocentric intellectual analysis of both man and society" spoken of here not surprisingly makes an allegorical representation of the Indian "noble world" much more compelling than what tribal people see as descriptive of living in the cultural reality.

Soyinka goes on to say that adoring the negro is as "sick" as abominating him, and certainly the recent love affair that the world has had with the American Indian (i.e., "new age-ism," etc.) is reaching fatuous, ridiculous, and, perhaps, the "sick" proportions of which Soyinka speaks. Few critics make the connection between what African intellectuals have to say about the white imagination in colonial literatures and what Indian writers contend. Both African and American Indian critics, however, including the Nobel Prize winner Soyinka, are often thought to be "propagandists" and the awareness (or fear) of this labeling may be what concerned Momaday as he wrote the review.[3] If one is brilliant enough, one can be an analyst, but often, in spite of the brilliance shown by African or Indian writers, they are still thought to be (secondarily, if nothing else) propagandists. To avoid that label and to avoid the argument, insipid clichés become useful.

Also, the desire to belong in this lost world described in Hill's novel sometimes results in an unthinking acceptance of the claim to authenticity without regard to accuracies in tribal knowledge, culture, and historical reality.[4] At the time of the novel's popularity (and little has changed in the two decades since then), a teacher from Columbus, Ohio, sent a letter to the *Indian Historian* journal in response to the nativist's criticism, posing authoritative pedagogical concerns:

I have been teaching a course entitled American Ethnic Literature at Capital University in Columbus, Ohio, and I confess to having been impressed with *Hanta Yo* despite its irritating tics of style and its leaden pace. What are the motives of a White teacher of Indian literature? Some possible motives occur to me: one is nostalgia for a lost world in which virtuous people lived in close harmony with nature and the holy; another is that a study of Indian history with its tale of betrayal and genocide is useful as a form of protest against oppression . . . [to] reveal the dark side of American History and give the lie to unqualified celebrations of the American Way; also, in an era of disillusionment with American values, many Americans are groping for new ones. What it all adds up to is that American Indians are called upon to prove some pet thesis.

Decades later, in the time of *Dances with Wolves*, many of these concerns still exist for Indians, even as American liberals without regard to the nativist struggle against colonialism continue to promote their own pet interests (i.e., Kevin Coster's childhood wish to be an Indian).

Resistance and opposition to the idea that subordinate or submerged cultures in America may be used to legitimize or understand failed American values, or unchanging Euro-American positions in history and scholarship, is ongoing in native enclaves, Indian-run schools and universities, and emerging Native American Studies departments in universities throughout the United States.

The non-Indian or nontribal intellectuals, then, in failing to become aware that the interests of submerged cultures have survived, and the memories of the grandmothers who were witnesses to outrage have informed the present story, are left to confront the irreconcilable elements and philosophical matters of their own cultures, remain in ignorance and fear, or become obstructionists to rival precepts. In the long run, issues of power and freedom of thought have always been a threat to established academic order, and the present situation is no exception.

This interesting defensive phenomenon has been described in D'Souza's now famous essay on "illiberal education," published in the *Atlantic Monthly* in 1991, which gave many examples of the struggle between professors and students in what he calls the effort "to transform liberal education in the name of minority victims." Putting the debate largely in terms of race rather than culture (i.e., black and white), he suggests that there is a "compromising of standards" and spends a good deal of time in the essay exploring the Duke University case in which that prestigious institution did not foresee what he says are the consequences of two of its recent decisions: (1) "to recruit professors who would make Duke a frontier for a 'new scholarship' in the humanities," and (2) "to bolster its preferential recruitment program for black faculty." The consequence, according to D'Souza has been "the end of meaning."

In the West, where native populations are large and sometimes visible, the debate centers more on how scholarship characterizes Indians, that is, the role of the academic expert as interpreter of non-Western culture, than on the issues of political correctness, or canon theory, or loss of meaning which D'Souza emphasizes, though there is an obvious connection.

Though it may seem redundant and irrelevant to most Indian faculty members and other intellectuals in their communities, Daniel F. Littlefield, Jr., a professor of English at the University of Arkansas at Little Rock, and the founder and (for the last decade) director of the National American Indian Press Archives at that institution, has argued publicly that native critics cannot and should not be summarily dismissed as condemnatory or restrictive. In a 1992 address to the

Mid-America American Studies Association meeting, entitled "American Indians, American Scholars, and the American Literary Canon," Littlefield agrees with those named by D'Souza who suggest that "we are on the verge of a revolution." Littlefield believes that the revolution in how white scholarship characterizes Indians is crucial to the current American scholarly debates. He points to the emerging academic voice of the Indian as the reason for the revolution in thought concerning curriculum and canon in the first place:

During the past twenty years, American Indians have been critical of American scholars, especially the anthropologists for whom their criticism has been relentless. How we respond to this question will determine in large measure how receptive Indian intellectuals will be to "new directions" in American Indian scholarship. We have steadily refused, they argue, to recognize Indians as colonized peoples. They see the strain on our relations as "a part of a worldwide phenomenon where tribal and other colonial people have challenged academic experts' role as interpreters of non-western cultures" and they accuse us of "lowering an ivory tower curtain around the exploitation and injustice suffered by subject or colonized peoples." (Buffalohead, "Self-rule in the Past and in the Future".) Thus, what we write has little to say about the realities of America as American Indians experience or have experienced them.[5]

Though he gives several examples of what he sees as change, he cautions that "for Indians, the spectre of appropriation remains."[6] And he cites the words of the Acoma Indian poet, Simon J. Ortiz, as follows:

There are a number of people who are utilizing indigenous cultures, not just Native American cultures but African Cultures. They use themes or characters, "Coyote" or Native American images which have a particular reference to philosophical and religious ceremonies which are very visual and so easily used, and oftentimes wrongly. And there has to be waged a struggle, and a very serious concern about misinformation and exploitation; exploitation means discrimination, racism and domination over subject peoples, subject cultures and languages.

These words by Ortiz were not uttered yesterday. They have been the thrust of his critical work as a creative artist for the better part of three decades. It is surprising how long it has taken for the native's voice to emerge in academia and imaginative thought. The emergence of this voice has little to do with the fear that the very concept of academic standards must be altered, though perhaps it must. It has less to do with the inaccuracies or simplistic views of cultural difference which are deplored as racist and politically correct or incorrect depending upon matters of taste, and even less to do with the fact that Western values have been inherently oppressive to native peoples. Its emergence has to do with the need of human beings to narrate, to tell the story of their own lives and the lives they have known, the intellectual need to inquire and draw conclusions which is simply a part of being human. Inevitably, if we take the human voice seriously, we must, as well, know that an historical and intellectual experience which required the exclusion of the Dakota grandmother from the public story is coercive, misguided, and meaningless.

The breaking of the native silence, then, the moving on from a Dakota grandmother's private remembrances, illustrates two realities. First, it illustrates the fact that history as written is quite different from history as it is lived, yet we must do what we can to write it. Second, it tells us that the imagination of each individual is quite unique, interesting, and exceptional, and it carries with it its own need to narrate.

Perhaps those of us who have been making the argument in recent years that individual works are comprehensible only within the context of the economic, behavioral, and political forces of the culture from which they emerge are simply pleading for cultural autonomy. It is a powerful argument and a poignant plea. Thoughtful American Indian critics do not see this argument as dangerous, hostile, or as a denial of history and art. In fact, they find that it is the most liberating reflection of all.

8

The American Indian Fiction Writers

Cosmopolitanism, Nationalism, the Third World, and First Nation Sovereignty

Cosmopolitanism

One of the observations made by Third World literary decolonization theoreticians like Homi K. Bhabha (Sussex), Timothy Brennan (Purdue), and perhaps a dozen other scholars even lesser known in the United States is that there are particular modern writers whose origins are not Euro-American, such as Salman Rushdie, Vargas Llosa, and perhaps Isabelle Allende and V. S. Naipaul, and (according to the Asian-American critic and novelist Frank Chin) even Amy Tan and Maxine Hong Kingston, who have moved away from the expected nationalistic affiliations towards an acquired "cosmopolitanism." In the process of doing so, it is argued, they have contributed to the confusion about cultural authority in the Third World literary voice.[1]

Little of analytical importance has been published about this confusion in cultural authority as it concerns the American Indian fiction writer, though in off-the-record discourse among scholars it is a critical interest. This essay begins by addressing what that observation means in terms of contemporary American Indian literatures and moves toward a broader analysis of nationalism in American Indian fiction. Explored within the contexts of Third World literary criticism will be the work of fiction writers who claim to be American Indians, those who are enrolled members (i.e., citizens) of existing tribal nations, and those who live the United States and write in English.

Third World intellectuals in discourse on nationalistic literatures, the theory of decolonizations in general, and cosmopolitanism in particular, argue that cosmopolitanism becomes the enemy of "resistance literatures" specifically because its criteria arise from Western tastes, or in other words, for aesthetic reasons. Specifically, according to Timothy Brennan, those criteria are as follows:

1. the preference, first of all, for novels (an imported genre), which sell better than poetry, testimonials, and plays even though the latter forms make up the majority of what is actually written in the Third World;

2. the tendency to privilege writing in European languages even though (in Asia and Middle East particularly) there are developed, continuous, and ancient literary traditions in such languages as Urdu, Bengali, Chinese, and Arabic;

3. the attraction to writing that thematises colonialism but that does not do so from a strident point of view; and, (in a way related to the last point)

4. the attraction to writing that is aesthetically "like us," that displays the complexities and subtleties of all "great art."

We may discuss the extent to which editors, publishers, and critics are involved in these preferences and attractions; however, the answer does not matter, for the writers themselves ultimately take responsibility for these trends. This means, of course, that the dialogue leading to the best understanding of the reality of fiction must be author-centered, a phenomenon not always evident in Native American literary studies and one which raises the questions of where these dialogues take place and for what audiences. For some world literatures, the *New York Times* occasionally offers examples of how helpful author-centered discussions concerning intent and responsibility can be. Recently it reported a conversation between Haruki Murakami and Jay McInerney in which Murakami says,

Yes, there is a sense of non-nationality about the story "Wind Up Bird and Tuesday's Woman," but it's not as though I depict Japanese society through that aspect of it that could just as well take place in New York or San Francisco. You might call it Japanese nature that remains only after you have thrown out, one after another, all those parts that are altogether too Japanese.

He is talking about cultural aesthetics; thus his intent in that context can then be explored. The fact that he writes fiction in the Japanese language does not make his authorial intent any more or any less a reality than it is for the American Indian writer who writes in English, except to make the odd point that Japanese is more accessible to critics, scholars, and readers than any Indian language in America. The reason it is not so easy for Native American writers to express intent in such discussions is that their work is almost always perceived as oriented toward a contrived "mainstream" (a function of colonialism) not only in publishing and editing but in critical analysis as well.

There is probably not an American Indian writer today who has not had questions of taste rather than intent posed as a prelude to publishing, such as "How can you make this story more accessible to the 'general American reader' "? (an agent's query) and "How and why is it that you use an Indian language word or phrase at certain places in your narrative, and don't you think you should have a glossary at the end of the manuscript?" (an editor's query). Such questions suggest that there is, in reality, an existing methodology which imposes a Euro-American cast upon the literary works of American Indian writers. "Stridency" in the native voice is also used to justify editorial intrusion, and comments like "editors took exception to your tone: far too much anger, sarcasm, and cynicism" are not unusual.

Native American writers, as a result of editorial and agented assistance in getting their manuscripts accepted, assume that under such strict circumstances their own efforts toward the recovery of memory through writing seem thwarted, selective, and narrowly interpreted within the imposed context of Western knowledge and aesthetics. Perhaps this is always the case in cross-cultural dialogue, but for American Indians whose work presumably stems from an obscure and "other" tribal perspective, any kind of postcolonial dialogue seems to be either of little interest to the mainstream or too strident.

A number of Native American writers have achieved broad readership either with or without this editorial intrusion. In light of this achievement and based on the preceding criteria, it is conceivable that Native American literary critics might ask whether successful American Indian writers, most notably Louise Erdrich, educated at Dartmouth College and a participant in the Johns Hopkins University Writing Program, and her husband, creative writer Michael Dorris (who make up the most popular writing team of the current era), as well as the nationally known Gros-Ventre/Blackfeet novelist, James Welch, the Kiowa intellectual N. Scott Momaday, and Laguna writer Leslie Marmon Silko may also have moved away from nationalistic concerns in order to gain the interest of mainstream readers. A number of lesser luminaries come to mind.

Few or perhaps none of these writers have ever claimed a major place as Third World thinkers, but they do speak out on issues both political and intellectual and are often considered experts in the field of Native American Studies and related topics, though some actively dislike that assumption by the non-Indian reading public. Close readings of their works by critics who are not interested in decolonization theories often suggest that these writers have an implied intimacy with the American Indian tribal experience.

These same critics, in assessing the work from a pedagogical standpoint, often claim for these writers a deeply authoritative cultural voice, a phenomenon which, in my view, clouds issues of intent and responsibility for Native American writers in the Third World lexicon. Thus, it appears that professors in Native American literatures, mostly white and male, have the capacity to rearrange native intellectualism in dubious ways. University of Montana professor Dr. William W. Bevins, for example, though perhaps not claiming to be a major pedagogue in the field, said in a recent article in the popular Washington Post publication *The World And I*, that Erdrich might be compared to William Faulkner, yet at the same moment tells us that she "sets the pace" as a foremost Native American Indian writer. In doing so, he unintentionally illustrates the confused status in critical theory and pedagogy of the nationalistic/cosmopolitan role as it applies to specific literary works. For those who have accepted the idea that Americans have a common literature, there is no problem. For those who want to pose the dialectics of difference, and that includes many American Indian writers, there are no options. Critics like Bevins, who want to have it both ways, are rarely challenged.

To be sure, Third World literary theorists are troubled by the lack of clear distinction between the nationalistic and cosmopolitan literary voice as a beginning point in the discussion of Native literatures because the strategy of ignoring and obscuring authorial intent lends itself to the pitting of pedagogical concerns and theoretical uses of literature against one another. The confusion largely stems from subject matter, the significant function of pedagogy. Because of what Erdrich writes about, says Bevins, and also because she is "Indian first and writer second," he claims for Erdrich and, by implication, for all others, a difference "from the mainstream American notion of defining ourselves by our vocation: a writer writes and can make any subject his own." The result is, Bevins posits, "that Indian writers are more like Third World writers, inherently political, marginal and social: serving their people." Being "like" Third World writers is, according to Bevins, as far as Erdrich goes.

Bevins's interest in the fact that Indian writers, including Erdrich, "don't even trespass on each other's tribes," much less attempt the range of material that most successful white writers take for granted as part of being "professional," suggests a "marginality" that is probably in no way an accurate assessment of the influence, popularity, and financial success of Erdrich and Dorris, especially considering the triblelessness of Dorris's *Yellow Raft In Blue Water*, and the sheer commercialism of *Crown of Columbus*.

To the extent that American Indian writers work with themes which might be said to be comparable to the themes of their contemporaries in the Third World, such as oppression, diaspora and displacement, colonization, racism, cultural conflict, exile, resistance, and other assorted experiences, their fiction brings several contingent arguments into focus not only for the writer and reader but for the critic as well. *Intent* is a large part of the failed discourse. Erdrich says unabashedly, "I am probably an Easterner who mistakenly grew up in the Midwest," thereby dismissing the essential notion of Native American intellectual knowledge, that is the reality of race memory as it is connected to environment and geography. How can one be a tribal nationalist and "set the pace" if one claims no connection to the land either in one's personal life or in one's fiction? One can't even say that this is a sentiment of the "exile," so pervasive in the writing of American Indians (for whom the journey theme is primary), nor of Third Worldists driven from their homelands.

This observation from a writer who is often thought by the scholarly public, perhaps mistakenly, to be doing nation-centered or tribal-centered (Chippewa) work adds to the confusion over defining the political realities of the function of Native literatures. The tacit worry that Native American writers are thought by critics and readers to be in some important way representative of modern tribal nationalistic perspective and the failure to be clear about authorial intent suggest several things about tribal sovereignty or First Nation status: that the tribes are not nations, that they are not part of the Third World perspective vis-à-vis colonialism, and that, finally, they are simply "colonized" enclaves in the United States, some kind of nebulous sociological phenomena. It is crucial to understand that such an assessment is in direct opposition not only to the historical reality of Indian nations in America, but also to the contemporary work being done by tribal governmental officials and activists, politicians, and grassroots intellectuals to defend sovereign definition in the new world.

Thus, the violation of nationalistic or Third World models in fiction and criticism should be of legitimate concern to scholars and should become part of the discourse in literary theory as it is applied to the works of Native American writers. While the writers themselves may disclaim any responsibility, and even while the critical, scholarly discussion is nonexistent or misdirected, the existence of such postcolonial incoherence on the part of writers who claim to be indigenous people can only contribute to the confusion about the role of minority intellectuals within the United States and, more important, their influence. Scholarship and art must say something about the real world, mustn't they? As Vine Deloria Jr., asked the anthropologists in 1970, "Where were you when we needed you?" Indians may now ask of their writers, two decades later, "Where were you when we defended ourselves and sought clarification as sovereigns in the modern world?"

In addition to authorial intent, themes of invasion and oppression so familiar to colonized peoples throughout the world that are taken up by American Indian writers serve as proof for the argument that major concerns of Third World theorists must be crucial analytical components of anything that might be said about the current literary trends in American Indian voice. These are themes about which mainstream critics can no longer be ignorant nor silent.

Themes and Aesthetics

In spite of Momaday's Pulitzer Prize and Erdrich's American Book Award, it is safe to say that the comparison of the success of these writers to the success of a global writer like Salman Rushdie, whose work has drawn the international spotlight, or Naipaul, one of the most prolific writers of our time, may seem inappropriate. Yet, their themes share a concern with the anticolonial struggle, intended or not. Thus, thematic similarities as well as tendencies toward European language and literary tastes would suggest that Brennan's "cosmopolitan" model, demonstrated by Rushdie in particular (perhaps not the best example, but surely a useful one) and described earlier in this essay, might have the same results if taken up by American Indian writers: first, the further obfuscation of the already confusing issues in the debate concerning the need for decolonization, that is, whether or not writers who claim to be indigenes are committed to the need for resistance; second, the relegation of the native writer to the status of an outsider, or even of a "traitor" (e.g., Rushdie); and third, the shying away of native writers from legitimate Third World points of view simply because they fear that their work will be labeled "strident," or lacking "artfulness," or "aesthetically flawed."

Without further examination of these literary realities, it is quite possible that American Indian writers will accept the notion that they can, and perhaps should, with impunity become cosmopolitans, serving as translators of materials into an already existing mode, or that they can and should legitimize "hybridity," or that they can and should transcend national affiliations, or that they can and should simply serve as "exotica." There seems to be evidence already that such influence is at work or thought to be at work in the public and scholarly assessment of the highly visible work of Erdrich and Dorris, *Crown of Columbus*, the publication so excellently planned and timed to coincide with the quincentennial of the "discovery" of America. The writers have been accused of everything from pandering to not living up to someone's expectations of them—comments which, first of all, suggest an unhealthy determinism but, more important, lead us away from discussions of decolonization in contemporary Native American Literatures.

Politics

The significance of the study of aesthetics and politics cannot be overemphasized, since American Indian fiction writers, clearly, have been instrumental, intentionally or not, in legitimizing the struggle to open up the American literary canon to include minority literatures, as though that were the major function of Third World writers. This effort may be appealing to some, especially in the face of the Bennett/Bloom hysteria that such an effort simply attempts to abolish the idea of canon altogether in American schools and is, therefore, almost treasonous. Even if the open-canon movement were to succeed, however, there remain for American Indian (First Nation) scholars two issues over which they will have little influence: first, opening up the canon is a little like opening world trade markets: exploitation abounds—a few legends here, a myth there. Seattle's famous oration, some poetry, and Momaday's "Man Made of Words" essay are inserted between the Age of Romanticism and T. S. Eliot just to illustrate some cross-cultural interest and fairness.

The second worry for the nativist is the question of whether or not opening up the American literary canon to include native literary traditions and contemporary works will have much relevance, given its own set of unique aims—the interest in establishing the myths and metaphors of sovereign nationalism; the places, the mythological beings, the genre structures and plots of the oral traditions; the wars and war leaders, the treaties and accords with other nations as the so-called gold standard against which everything can be judged. These are the elements of nationalism which have always fueled the literary canon of tribal peoples and their literary lives. In my own tribal literary traditions, there is a fairly long list of Dakota/Lakota writers and storytellers as well as a huge body of ritual and ceremony against which everything may be compared. Reference to the body of nationalistic myths, legends, metaphors, symbols, historical persons and events, writers and their writings must form the basis of the critical discourse that functions in the name of the people; the presence of the Indian nation as cultural force a matter of principle.

The unfortunate truth is that there are few significant works being produced today by the currently popular American Indian fiction writers which examine the meaningfulness of indigenous or tribal sovereignty in the twenty-first century. Seemingly overwhelmed by violence, self-hate, romanticism, blame, mournfulness, loss, or anger, the writers seem to suggest that there is little room for liberation literature, little use for nationalistic/tribal resistance. Frank Chin's observation that in the case of Asian works, history was nearly destroyed by Christian missionaries and is now being faked by writers continuing in that tradition must be taken up by Native American critics as a cause-and-effect probability.

The Christian-oriented apocalyptic vision of Erdrich's rich prose, the anguished dismissal of the nationhood of the Blackfeet by James Welch, the ambiguity concerning the Indian rights struggle of politics and land in my own novel, the mythic self-absorption of Scott Momaday, perhaps even the feeling that "whoever wants to be tribal can join the tribe" of Gerald Vizenor (and we could, perhaps, name a dozen more) collectively seem to leave American Indian tribal peoples in this country stateless, politically inept, and utterly without nationalistic alternatives. The idea that Indians lacked political skills, which may now have found its way into contemporary fiction written by Indians, is a stereotype which has been used by historians for a century to dismiss and distort early Indian/white relations. Though Gerald Vizenor has described my recent long fiction, *From the River's Edge*, as a novel which "celebrates the honorable conditions of tribal sovereignty and survivance," there is an intellectual uncertainty in its whole which is an appalling and unexpected flaw in the imaginative work of a daughter of tribal politicians, men and women for whom there was no ideological ambivalence concerning nationhood. In characterization, at least, I simply tell you about a believer; Tatekeya has faith. He believes, and because faith is complete in itself, he cannot respond to secular divisiveness. He has no rules for modern politics, only a degree of faith. While Tatekeya may be attempting to say how it is that he may return to a moral world, the reality of our real lives as tribal people is that without effective politics, such a return can be at best temporary.

Nationalism

At a time when nationalism seems to be asserting itself in the world in new and puzzling ways, the most obvious example being the breakaway republics of the former U.S.S.R., the people of America's First Nations find themselves struggling with the myths of their own national status against a long history of enforced denationalization. Yet the American Indian writers who have achieved successful readership in mainstream America seem to avoid that struggle in their work and present Indian populations as simply gatherings of exiles, emigrants, and refugees, strangers to themselves and their lands, pawns in the control of white manipulators, mixed-bloods searching for identity—giving support, finally, the idea of nationalistic/tribal culture as a contradiction in terms.

The work of traditional native thinkers like the Lakota religious leader Arvol Looking Horse, Sioux attorneys Mario Gonzalez and Vine Deloria Jr., politicians such as Birgil Kills Straight, members of the Grey Eagles Society, Alex White Plume, and countless other individuals and institutions with First Nation status suggest otherwise. The organizers of the 1985–1990 Big Foot Ride Centennial from Fort Yates, North Dakota, to Wounded Knee, South Dakota (in ceremonial grieving of the death of over three hundred unarmed Lakotas), the ever-present tribal orators who concern themselves with healing the Sioux Nation's wounds, and the hundreds of others involved in such continuing tribal activities throughout the country illustrate the historical interest in decolonization and the revival of nationalistic paradigms necessary for the return of the spirit and the journey into the twenty-first century.

These matters are often looked upon as the fanciful emergence of empire building which exists isolated from the literary voice of the people, or else they are dismissed as mere political action for political gain and dangerous authoritarianism. However, if they are examined as essentially literary events, actions, and ideas, it may be that the incorporation of such concrete praxis can affect canon theory and literary theory (as it always has in oral societies) by challenging intellectual orthodoxies which do not appreciate—indeed, negate and omit—a nationalistic approach to the development and interpretation of any works, including contemporary fiction.

In this current movement of critical thought away from Europeanism, native traditionalists are telling scholars it is time to abandon the idea that without pope or emperor nationhood has never been achieved, that, on the contrary, national affiliations are a part of the urgency of contemporary thought and writing for American Indians, whose own national histories have never been appropriately defined in reality-based, historical contexts. It is the challenge of modern thinkers and critics to find out what these nativist ideals mean in terms of the function of literature.

Many of today's scholars are willing to make that move, though they may not know how, and their freedom to do so may be stifled by a body of inchoate reasoning called empirical criticism. This means that they are often fearful of exacting a decolonizing focus and thus refuse to enter the discourse wholeheartedly. Writer and critic Raymond Williams, for example, in his very interesting and forward-looking book, *The Year 2000*, though drifting toward a global focus rather than a tribal one, unintentionally reasserts the native view in this limited way: " 'Nation' as a term is radically connected with native. We are born into relationships which are typically settled in a place. This form of primary and 'placeable' bonding is of quite fundamental human and natural importance."

American Indians couldn't agree more. However, Williams concludes that the jump from that to anything like the modern nation-state is entirely artificial. His refusal to take up the function of the indigenous myths of origin on this continent, which are irrevocably tied to place and tribal nationalism makes his conclusion seem both racist and nonfunctional. He further asserts the colonist view in America and does little to clarify the reality of national existence as it has applied to the modern treaty-status tribes (the First Nation) in the United States and Canada for at least a hundred years and, traditionally, for thousands more.

While intellectual antagonists have always existed in the fight for American Indian nationhood, tribal bonding with geography as the most persistent native nationalistic sentiment is often dismissed as a major criterion for nationhood in the modern world. Recognition of the need for decolonization inherent in a people's spiritual connection to the land rises from history and mythology, two components of literature; yet, scholarly awareness of the corrupt thinking which disavows this criterion emerges from wildly dissimilar theorists. Ernest Renan, for example, the nineteenth-century French philosopher, surely removed from the experience of the natives in the so-called wilds of America, delivered a lecture at the Sorbonne in 1882 in which he defined a nation in this way:

A nation is a soul, a spiritual principle. Two things, which in truth are but one, constitute this soul or spiritual principle. One lies in the past, one in the present. One is the possession in common of a rich legacy of memories; the other is present day consent, the desire to live together, the will to perpetuate the value of the heritage that one has received in an undivided form. Man does not improvise. The nation, like the individual, is the culmination of a long past of endeavors, sacrifices, and devotions.

This lecture was delivered as the Indian nations of North America were in the final stages of a bloody war in defense of their lands and sovereign rights. On the northern plains and throughout much of America, the wars ended in peace treaties signed between sovereigns. Much of Renen's argument is found in all of the works of American Indians then and now, and it may even constitute part of the rationale for the common trait Bevins points out when he says of American Indian writers today, "They don't even trespass upon each other's tribes." Surely, there is a sense of loyalty to that ideal in all of the writers mentioned in this discussion (for some more than others).

Unfortunately, Renan's discourse turns out to be an argument for colonization rather than the nationalism which indigenous peoples have imagined and asserted for generations, for he goes on to dismiss race, language, religion, and geography as anything more than natural considerations: "It is no more soil than it is race which makes a nation. The soil furnishes the substratum, the field of struggle and of labor; man furnishes the soul. Man is everything in the formation of this sacred thing which is called a people."

The indigenous view of the world—that the very origins of a people are specifically tribal (nationalistic) and rooted in a specific geography (place), that mythology (soul) and geography (land) are inseparable, that even language is rooted in a specific place—make Renan's considerations antagonistic to the kind of discourse on nationalism desired by American Indian intellectuals.

The broad acceptance of Renan's one-sided arguments in American intellectual thought has lessened the tensions for American Indian writers (themselves constantly subjected to colonization and assimilation forces), and the result is they may no longer feel hostile nor isolated from modernity and cosmopolitanism. They begin to feel that decolonization may be both ridiculous and irrelevant besides being impossible and futile. They no longer know what the Hunkpapa Sioux Chieftain Sitting Bull meant when he said, "God made me an Indian and he put me here, *in this place*." It seems to them very much like Mormonism, perhaps, or any cultish view. The term *nationalism*, then, takes on a pejorative definition except to such unique critics as the Osage professor of English

and Native Studies, Dr. Robert Warrior, now at Stanford, who says that
the work of criticism is not to pronounce judgments but to "go beyond
merely invoking categories and engage in careful exploration of how
those categories impact the process of sovereignty."

Euro-American scholars have always been willing to forego discussion concerning the connection between literary voice and geography
and what that means to Indian nationhood. It is with regard to this
failure that Warrior's challenge is particularly meaningful.

Reality of the Third World and Tribal Sovereignty

What Third Worldists, then, have in common is the question of what
their fictive mythmaking has to do with the reality of their postcolonial
conditions as *nations* of people. For those writers who are called American Indians, the question of whether the myth of nationhood is a cultural
force is often unanswerable in their works. The idea that a national
culture exists for them is obliterated by ideas of minority status in
the United States, temporality, dysfunction, Indian-ness. The sovereign
rights and obligations of citizens of the First Nation of America as
modern concepts seem less important to today's writers than stories
of loss, exile, identity, and degeneration.

If it is true, as the Palestinian critic Professor Edward W. Said asserts,
that the " 'nationalistic mood' is aesthetically and socially more strongly
felt in the emergent societies of the world today," (and, therefore, one
assumes, in the struggling colonized societies), the question for native
writers of fiction becomes, To what extent does my specific contemporary tribal voice mirror that strongly felt idea? And, specifically, how
does that passion realize itself within the content or plot of a given
novel? or does it? or need it? The question for critics is, Have we shown
a lack of interest in this surge, and have we failed to apply Third World
critical methodology to major works?

Perhaps the most ambitious novel yet published by an American
Indian fiction writer which fearlessly asserts a collective indigenous
retrieval of the lands stolen through colonization is Leslie Marmon
Silko's *Almanac of the Dead*, published in 1992. The idea of decolonization,
Silko tells us, is dependent upon writing that has "living power within it,
a power that would bring all the tribal peoples in the Americas together
to retake the land." She obviously clings to the idea that the imagination
plays a functional role in political and social life, an idea which most of
the native traditionalists I have known have always held.

Silko's new novel seems to stand alone in creating a fictionalized pantribal nationalism, an event which provides an interesting, antagonistic, rebellious moment in contemporary literary development. In that light, it seems difficult to explain the hostile reaction to her critical analysis of the work of other writers. Her assessment of Louise Erdrich's work, in particular, is seen by some as an attack, rather than as a sincere effort to understand the forces which have served to displace the discussion of the nation as a cultural force in literature. Louis Owens, in *Other Destinies*, charges Silko with an "attack" upon Erdrich's *Beet Queen*, which she calls "a strange artifact, an eloquent example of the political climate in America in 1986." Owens says,

Oddly, in attacking the book for its refusal to foreground the undeniably bitter racism toward Indians in America's heartland Silko seems to be demanding that writers who identify as Indian, or mixedblood, must write rhetorically and polemically, a posture that leaves little room for the kind of heterogeneous literature that would reflect the rich diversity of Indian experiences, lives and cultures . . . and a posture Silko certainly does not assume in her own fiction.

If a native artist's effort to examine forms of narrative which do or do not express the ideology of the modern nation, which is a major concern of Third World criticism and the real focus of Silko's comments on Erdrich's work, is labeled as an "attack" by presumably knowledgeable critics, then the ability of American Indians to create new forms of living and writing is seriously jeopardized.

Owens is quite wrong about Silko's posture, at least as far as it applies to her most recent novel, *Almanac of the Dead*, for it is the foremost Indian novel in which we see the clear and unmistakable attempt to describe Indian nationalism in what she sees as modern terms. That diagnosis of native nationalism, which appears in terms of economics, power, and numbers, however troubling to the moralists among us, attempts to redefine the boundaries of the Western hemisphere, and is strangely familiar to the militants of the last decades and haunting to anyone who understands the longing of a tribal nation for its homelands.

Retribution, a major part of that nationalism, is obviously a matter of utmost importance to Silko, to indigenous peoples everywhere and, in particular, to people like the citizens of the Sioux Nation who are presently engaged in the longest legal struggle for the return of stolen lands (the Paha Sapa) in the history of the United States. You need only look at the current and historical legislative efforts of tribal people, the contemporary speeches of people like Royal Bull Bear, Arvol Looking Horse, and the now-deceased Fools Crow (Eagle Bear); you need only look at the body of oratory by American Indians in history, the continued ritual life in native communities, and the work of the International Indian Treaty Organizations to understand that the political reality of the imagination, as Silko's work suggests, is a major component of nationalism.

Silko's novel, however, in describing America's worst nightmare, that is, the triumph of the indigenes as tidal waves of South and North American Indians wipe out borders and reclaim lands, does not answer all of the prayers of the First Nation purists just named. These purists, by and large, have not moved away from the traditional stance of their own tribal legacies, nor from the 1970s "awakening" spoken of by Said when Third Worldists had not yet been labeled "people of color" in lieu of their own nationalistic/tribal titles and definitions. Thus, the unanswered questions of a privileged Third World author, separated from the realities she describes (a condition found almost everywhere in the Third World), support two tendencies in nation-centered fiction: they temper but do not refute the sweeping claims of her fiction that imagination is the source of history, an ambiguity of some importance to scholars. More important, they reassure readers and critics that the process of authenticating cultural interpretation for American Indians is ongoing. Both of these tendencies must be acknowledged in the critical work which will inevitably accompany the developing body of contemporary American Indian fiction.

While what has happened in critical discourse may be confusing and inappropriate, the pedagogical debate centered upon multiculturalism in the United States is no less chaotic. In practice, multicultural education has not and will not cast much light on the centuries-long struggle for sovereignty faced by the people of the First Nation of America. Its very nature, ironically, is in conflict with the concept of American Indian sovereignty, since it emphasizes matters of spirituality and culture, anthropology and sociology.

Laguna author, critic, and professor, Paula Gunn Allen has taken up the issue of literature and notions of tribal sacred reality and privacy as related to pedagogy in her recent essay, "Special Problems in Teaching Leslie Marmon Silko's *Ceremony*" though she, too, avoids the discussion of nation-centered scholarship in that essay. Gunn-Allen says she tends to "non-teach" *Ceremony* because she finds it particularly troublesome:

I focus on the story, the plot and action. I read the novel quite differently from how it is read by many, I believe. I could no more do (sanction) the kind of ceremonial investigation of *Ceremony* done by some researchers than I could slit my mother's throat. Even seeing some of it published makes my skin crawl. I have yet to read one of those articles all the way through, my reaction is so pronounced.

I teach the novel as being about a half-breed, in the context of half-breed literature from *Cogewea* on. Certainly, that is how I read the novel the first time I read it, as a plea for inclusion by a writer who felt excluded and compelled to depict the potential importance of breeds to Laguna survival. The parts of the novel that set other pulses atremble largely escaped me. The long poem text that runs through the center has always seemed to me to contribute little to the story or its understanding. Certainly, the salvation of Laguna from Drought is one of its themes, but the Tayo stories which, I surmise, form their own body of literature would have been a better choice if Silko's intentions were to clarify or support her text with traditional materials.

Tayo is the name of one of the dramatic characters around Keres-land. Perhaps in some story I am unfamiliar with, he is involved with Fly or Reed Woman. But, the story she lays alongside the novel is a clan story and is not told outside the clan.

I have long wondered why she did so. Certainly, being raised in greater proximity to Laguna Village than I, she must have been told what I was, that we don't tell those things outside. Perhaps her desire to demonstrate the importance of breeds led her to do this, or perhaps no one ever told her why the Lagunas and other Pueblos are so closed about their spiritual activities and the allied oral tradition.

Putting these matters in the context of pedagogy as Gunn-Allen does suggests very clearly the heretofore unspoken risks of omission and distortion in the opening up of the canon, in some ways resembling the contradictory role played by Salman Rushdie's literary contributions to global and American fiction.

The opening up of the canon, an American democratic ideal so vigorously pursued by scholars, writers, and professors like Dr. Paul Lauter whose interests in open admissions policies, women's studies, and black studies have fostered in the last two decades a movement of great force, unintentionally belittles the very real conflict between what Third Worldists call "national form" and "anticolonial liberalism," which is really at the heart of the Rushdie tragedy. Gunn-Allen's comments here on Silko illustrate the dilemma for American Indians.

While the point about pedagogy that Gunn-Allen makes concerning *Ceremony* might also be true of Silko's earlier works (for example, the short fiction *Tony's Story*, in contrast to the Simon J. Ortiz rendering of the same event in *The Killing of a State Cop*), the real issue here is that canon theory and critical theory rise out of pedagogy, not the other way around, as some have suggested, thereby magnifying issues of cultural authenticity. Since, in general, the faculties in departments where these works are taught are often the last places to draw in any great numbers of Native scholars, it is quite likely that conflicting and minority views will be dismissed, distorted, or unknown.

Whatever may be said about Silko's earlier works, *Almanac of the Dead* engages in and insists upon the nationalist's approach to historical events and in the process seems to put any so-called pandering ordinarily required of the storyteller in its place. Her effort here in her new work is to create a pan-Indian journey toward retribution, not to appeal to nonindigenous mainstream readership nor to tell tribal secrets.

While this is a heartening focus, it too fails in this nationalistic approach, since it does not take into account the specific kind of tribal/nation status of the original occupants of this continent. There is no apparatus that allows the tribally specific treaty-status paradigm to be realized either in Silko's fiction or in the pan-Indian approach to history. The explanation for that in tribal terms may be that Laguna falls under the Treaty of Guadalupe Hidalgo—very different circumstances from the Plains Indian Treaty paradigm. Nonetheless, if it is true that the definition of a nation is historically determined, then Silko's vision might seem unworkable or even offensive to those nation-states that insist upon the accuracy of their own specific histories. Her gallant effort, though, makes us realize that the theories, both literary and spiritual, about the world in which American Indians find themselves are not to be abandoned by the literati.

The pedagogical problems referred to by Gunn-Allen take many forms, and they most often have to do with discussion of the intent of the works themselves and the intent of their traditions. It seems sensible to point out in an instance or two what happens when interpretations of the literature of the Sioux, for example, are almost always rendered in English by non-Sioux scholars in the pedagogical mode. The continuous overtracing of personal histories within the *tiospaye* concept (defined as a societal/cultural/tribal organizational construct), which is based upon blood and ancestral ties and lineage and is so much a part of the storytelling process for the Sioux, is never put into the Third World theoretical lexicon simply because the professors are not much interested or are uninformed. The result is the diminishment or alteration of the *tiospaye* concept *as a nationalistic forum* for the people, in spite of the fact that the appropriate interpretation of traditional literatures suggests that nationalism is a major reason for their existence. Pedagogical models rising out of anthropology departments and literary/humanistic study centers are almost entirely responsible for this phenomenon. Since pedagogical models are rarely criticized within the Third World theoretical framework, the literatures themselves are rarely conceptualized as foundations for native political insight and action, and the result is that the study of their own literatures by tribal people becomes irrelevant to their lives.

One example of the lack of critical sensitivity for Third World concerns is Julian Rice's work on the Ella Deloria materials in Sioux literatures. Ms Deloria's *Dakota Texts*, translation studies in language and literature first published in the early decades of this century, an exemplary tribal work by a tribal scholar, has become the basis for much subsequent scholarship in Lakota/Dakota/Nakota (i.e., Sioux) literatures.

Rice, in his work *Lakota Storytelling* (1988) embellishes the notion of Dr. Raymond DeMallie, considered a foremost scholar in Sioux religions, that "real kinship" (which is a major function of the *tiospaye*) was not narrowly defined by the Lakotas in biological terms, but was defined, rather, by behavior. "Even today, among the Lakotas," DeMallie asserts, "relatives are people who act like relatives and consider themselves to be related." There is little understanding that while this is, of course, accepted as a philosophical idea, behavior alone does not make one a Lakota. One cannot be a Lakota unless one is related by the lineage (blood) rules of the *tiospaye*. While it is true that the narrow definition of biology was not accepted by the Lakotas, since they are also related to the animal world, spirit world, and everything else in the world, biology is *never* dismissed categorically. On the contrary, it is the overriding concern of the people who assiduously trace their blood ties throughout the generations.

This ambiguity, further asserted through the literary studies of Rice, seems to extend anthropological theories which may define the Lakota as a sociological phenomenon rather than in terms of the political lexicon of the nationhood of people who know their citizenship to be based upon the blood kinship rules of lineage inherent in the *tiospaye*. They are citizens of a sovereign nation that signed treaties with the United States of America and, before that, defended and allied themselves throughout history with the citizens of other tribal nations.

The implication of these mostly pedagogical studies by the foremost white male scholars in the field is profoundly disturbing. The idea that *if you act like a Lakota you are a Lakota*, seeming to emerge from their genuine if misguided interest in putting Ella Deloria's work to good classroom use, is patently absurd to the people who call themselves Lakotas. The end result is even more devastating, since the sincere pedagogical efforts to bring this material into contemporary classrooms seem to have resulted in the creation of a body of critical work which renders the literature useless to the people from whom it originates. It is particularly ironic that Rice uses the Blood-Clot stories, essential as origin stories of the people, to demonstrate his obvious thesis, which is as follows:

As a microcosm of a family united in strength and natural affection rather than by blood, the Lakota learn that proper identity and attitude.

Kinship between human beings or between animal spirits and human beings is determined by love and behavior rather than blood.

Nowhere in his examination of the Deloria work, in which he also discusses Black Elk and Fools Crow materials, does he clarify this over-simplified position. In addition to being simply absurd, the question of what such omissions might be contributing to the current controversies concerning the New Age "becoming Indian" fad so offensive to Indian populations remains to be answered. Rice's work, originally published by subsidiary presses, is now being taken up and published by other more orthodox university presses.

While this discussion does not intend to present Rice's work as totally corrupt, it is used here to illustrate how ludicrously inappropriate much scholarship is to the nationhood status of Indian America. When white scholars articulate a private vision with little or no interest in understanding the national conscience, their voices seem shamefully inauthentic. This fact, however, is rarely perceived by other, similarly uninformed scholars, readers, and professors.

Some of Rice's other conclusions are equally astonishing, even in studies of a less esoteric mode such as the contemporary oratory of the Sioux. He misinterprets the unifying motif of a speech by Fools Crow as "giving." Listening to the speech, Lakota, on the other hand, believe the unifying motif to be "sharing." This is a long-standing issue in interpretation made public in preliminary studies of others who precede Dr. Rice, namely the work of Dr. John Bryde, a former priest, who wrote on Indian values and attempted to clarify them some two decades ago when he taught courses in Indian psychology at the University of South Dakota. Lakota listeners, supposing a past in which the nation has suffered and that any understanding requires a common effort, know that nationhood for the Lakota is based on sharing, of which giving is only a part. To claim otherwise is to misunderstand the nationalistic function of oratory as a literary genre in the study of native literatures and reciprocity as a major principle of the *tiospaye* concept.

In conclusion, then, I suggest that pedagogical works in tribal literatures be critiqued within Third World theoretical considerations more than they are at present. The interest in decolonization goes back to the Mayan resistance narratives of the 1500s and has always played an important role in political and social life.

Tribal scholars like my fellow tribeswoman Ella Deloria, as well as all the subsequent fiction writers and scholars mentioned in this article and many others not mentioned, have stumbled into this remarkable debate about society and culture. The climate in which these debates occur is fraught with risk because it appears that much of what is called contemporary American Indian fiction and scholarship is validated as such by non-Indian publishers, editors, critics, and scholars for reasons which have very little to do with the survival into the twenty-first century of the First Nation of America.

Because of flaws in pedagogy and criticism, much modern fiction written in English by American Indians is being used as the basis for the cynical absorption into the "melting pot," pragmatic inclusion in the canon, and involuntary unification of an American national literary voice. Ironically, much of the criticism and fiction published today contributes to the further domination of modern nations and individualism, all the while failing in its own implied search for sovereignty and tribalism. To succumb to such an intellectual state is to cut one's self off as a Native American writer from effective political action. It severs one's link not only to the past but to the present search by one's native compatriots for legitimate First Nation status.

Part Four

WOMEN'S LIVES

9

The American Indian Woman in the Ivory Tower

Until recent decades, Native American women probably gave little thought to the idea that societal and professional status was achieved or denied on the basis of gender. Sex difference, so far as we know, was a "given" in tribal life and, often, the roles and status of the two sexes in the community seemed not to be a matter of conflict or ambiguity. Indeed, it may still seem so for many of us who recognize that more central to tribal thinking are the matters of individual choice and preference, personal dignity, privacy, industry, competence, political issues, treaty rights, litigation, and sovereignty—all significant considerations in rather egalitarian cultures developing tribalistically.

As we move out of tribal societies, however, and as we take up the issues of nontraditional lifestyles which are now so much a part of modern Indian ways even on Indian homelands, the subject of women's roles both in the context of mainstream American life and in tribal life, becomes more challenging. One of the consequences, as we know, of the coercive assimilation policies of the 1950s and 1960s, now called the Termination/Relocation Era, is that more than 50 percent of all American Indians now live away from their tribal homelands and societies.

For Indian women as well as Indian men, this fact of life has challenged traditional tribalism, and the adjustment to such drastic changes now requires thoughtful consideration of our lives in concert. It is a fact of contemporary American life that men and women everywhere in the modern world are examining conflicts and developments concerning gender roles that are historical and cultural in nature. Native men and women join in this examination.

Thus, we ask, What is an appropriate female role in modern Indian society? How do we interact with our male counterparts? our husbands? fathers? brothers? professional male colleagues? What are the consequences of acquiring educational skills, advanced degrees, and employment to our culture, to our tribes? Who will our children be? What is the role of scholarship and academic participation in native life? How may Indian women either support or deny their historical legacies and what are the personal consequences of each? Even more personally, what may Indian women and men expect of one another?

All of these questions and many others are important for Indian people, and today they are especially significant for the Indian woman at the university level in the educational system, the Indian woman in the "ivory tower," so to speak. She is the woman who has become, by her own choice, a participant in the work of the academic centers of this country.

The answers to these questions will come, at least in part, from the past historical experience of other native women. What a modern Indian woman in the 1990s is doing is very likely dependent upon what her female ancestors and relatives, have done. She walks the road smoothed for her by the women who preceded her. She does not, contrary to public opinion, operate in a vacuum, and she is not without precursors. Today's native women often do not claim as their heroines those women whose virtues have been extolled by whites. Sacajawea, for example, who led Lewis and Clark across the mountains, whose statue often stands in the rose gardens of museums and universities, is not universally seen by contemporary Indian women as a figure to be emulated. She led the whites into her country, married the Frenchman Charbonneau, and died in childbirth. In tribal history, she did nothing to assure the survival of her people. Today's native women often cannot even claim each other, since they often live in isolation from any tribal connection at various universities and other job sites.

Now and again when I think about this I'm moved to try to say something about the women who have influenced me, and most often they are not people who have gained reputations through the white man's history, nor are they even those women of the newer generations who, since the turn of the century, have achieved intellectual status. I have a tendency to speak more often of the women who tended my childhood, though they usually did not seek success in modern school systems, nor did they even speak the English language. When I wrote a poem about the grandmother mentioned earlier in this work, she became an archetypal heroine. This is what I said:

First the Loon Dived:

Grandmother, born a hundred years after the U. S. Constitution was written, years before Alexander Graham Bell invented the telephone, from the beginning a reluctant heiress to too much land where exit signs posted by the invaders and tales of solitude in another world appeared in lucid dreams; we come, you and I, from the wide, lush prairie lands and woods of the northeast to the cramped bottomlands at Crow Creek where the ground is always damp and reptiles rise from weeds to drive for the flesh of intruders.

Grandmother, today your landscape is light pursuing light, forever a human mirror in memory unblemished and close to the heart; when I walk to your place from the flat prairie above I can depend on your horses fraught with the destiny of us all following me through the dark discovering my presence. As if by instinct, we pause; feeling the primal warmth of their hot breath I slow down to let them pass, nyctalopia and night mist my only companions. I feel my way, unseeing and alone. Huge cottonwoods and elms along the creekbed extinguish any light that may reflect off the water and the landscape that haunts me even in darkness or fictional guise tells me outside on a prairie knoll there is a secret world:

> Men carry the buffalo skull
> on a bed of sage
> and face away from the tree.

Timeless, eternal light flows only from the earth and the inner riches of your snow-capped years. You never promised me dark thickets nor lightning flashes of the death journey attached by a mere faint rainbow to the monsters of the other side.

So the Muskrat Dived:

Though the Agency town still called the Heart of the Crow does nothing to enoble the indifference of a long and troubled history, we learn how to be born; long-winded, powerful underwater, the muskrat carried a fragment of mud in his claw and we went West, off-hand, dizzy in the moment, and there, alone, we learned to be Dakotas, slaying the dogs to be thrown into the great waters for the spirits, vanishing beneath the surface to reassure in mortal time our timelessness. Rare evenings when sleep won't come we sit in lamplight. We listen to the screech of the night owl and watch for Sputnik. We talk of apostates and the price we paid. Funeral processions are only for the dead, you say to me.

The woman of this poem was, one supposes, a keeper of myth in the traditional sense.[1] She taught her language to her babies, and she told the stories. The influence of such women upon one another has been speculated upon only rarely by scholars, and they have been outsiders. Much of the good research about these women and their influences will come, I predict, from the native women themselves, tribal women and even those of us in the ivory towers of American universities, for we yearn to know more of these women, these keepers of myth.

The educational experiences of the women spoken of here as archetypal, the mothers and grandmothers of all of us, were different from ours, the chief difference being that their participation in the white man's educational system was most likely coerced in ways that ours was not. Most of us, unlike our predecessors, have become a part of the ivory tower by choice; few of us have been confronted with the intensive effort to coercively assimilate Indians into modern society that was the pattern in the latter part and at the turn of the nineteenth century. Hampton, Carlisle, Genoa, Rapid City, Phoenix, and countless other places were gasping a last breath by the time we came along. While we went with our brothers to off-reservation boarding schools, it was really never the same thing.

At the turn of the century, the secretary of Interior, Carl Shurz, an influential reformer who believed that American Indian women were vital cogs in the machine of assimilation and that it was the function of an educated (i.e., "civilized") Indian woman to know how to make beds, sew, cook "the American way," and scrub floors, could not have imagined our emergence as directors of programs, museum officials, doctoral candidates, researchers, teachers, and professors. He would be disappointed in us, perhaps, because we have rejected the role he saw for us as an Indian husband's helpmate as he disappeared into the American mainstream.

The fact of this different history, however, has caused American Indian women to make decisions about traditions and transitions which have proven to be exacting, compelling, and sometimes tragic, for many of the women of these past historical periods really did disappear into the American mainstream along with their families and never again returned to their homelands and reservations. Or, if they did, they had become so influenced by an alien lifestyle that they were not any longer considered useful repositors of tribal concerns, hopes, and plans, as they had once been. Many of them, though not all, were no longer the "keepers of myth." Many of them contributed, then, to a situation of assimilation in academia that we all still find ourselves in and though we may have achieved reasonable success in our endeavors, we ask, What is my role as an American Indian woman who has achieved advanced degrees in the white man's academic disciplines, and what is my responsibility to my community?

There are few easy answers.

As female heirs to a legacy of enforced assimilation, we should probably begin to examine our academic lives within the parameters not only of the history spoken of here but also of culture, that is, the philosophical, spiritual and experiential guidelines of the traditional worlds of tribalism. Those of us born and raised on reservations in this century as I was have the dubious distinction of being influenced by some of the most important cyclical events in modern history: the Indian Reorganization Act, the relocation and termination laws, and self-determination. We remember these events and we know that the cycle completes itself and begins again and again. We know that the pendulum swings, and throughout it all, Indian nations continue the struggle for sovereignty and self-determination.

We remember being told of the 1930s and 1940s when our parents and grandparents who had survived the Christianizing and Extermination Eras of the previous century began the struggle again for cultural survival in a national climate of renewed interest in what has come to be called Indian Reorganization, a tentative period which most survivors recognized as respite from a hundred years of genocide. We remember the assault upon our cultures and histories as the pendulum swung back to the Termination/Relocation Era of the 1950s. The pressure to cut our hair, move to the cities of America, and marry nontribal men because such a marriage would make our lives easier and more efficient was enormous. We entered university life far away from our homelands. Sometimes we were the first women of our tribes to receive academic degrees from a university, but not, we should have known, the first women of our tribes to accept or reject the responsibility for ourselves, and for tribal people and our relatives. *The extent to which we resisted the pressures thrust upon us during those times is, I believe, the extent to which we have been successful in acquiring leadership roles in modern Indian society. And it has been a difficult half century.*

Some interesting patterns of how Native American women, especially the women of the northern plains, gained or failed to gain recognition, that is, power and status, emerged from the historical experiences of the nineteenth century. For the women who, after schooling, did not return to the reservations, for the women who ignored traditional marriage patterns by marrying nontribal men, for the women whose children no longer represented the bloodlines of the tribes, the matter of claiming intellectual, spiritual, or social leadership roles was complicated and difficult. They often became useful only as they served to further and support assimilationist views and were often regarded with suspicion by others in the tribe.

On the other hand, the women who did return to the reservations to take up tribal lives following off-reservation educational experiences discovered they had two options. They could succumb to a pervasive anti-intellectualism which prevailed in reservation life, and perhaps still does to some degree, as a defensive stance spawned by the reality that education was used as an assimilation device. This meant that they would ignore or reject intrusions inherent in the process of change to become a kind of silent majority, unheard from and largely unknown. Or, they could become active in the white man's bureaucracies, churches, schools, governments, in order to have a modicum of influence over the inevitable changes which would occur with or without the consent of the people.

Those who chose to give in to the anti-intellectualism of the times often lived in poverty, resisted sending their children to school, did not teach nor aspire to positions of authority within the educational and governmental apparatuses available to them. Their energies often went into homemaking, gardening, and the underground activities which surrounded a hidden ritual life of tradition and tribal religious practice. They bore children and eventually became the respected grandmothers, pillars of sometimes stable but oftentimes unstable families, caught in the confusion of enforced transition but not fully participating in it. Some became victims and lived in dread and desperation. These were the women who were caught up in the either/or dichotomy of modern Indian life: either traditional, or modern, either Indian or white, full-blood insider or mixed-blood outsider. They often saw nothing in between those polarized position, and they saw no way out.

Conversely, those women who chose to become active in the white man's world established on reservations by the federal government were often rejected by their own communities. Marriage partnerships with members of so-called traditional families were often impossible. As a result they sometimes entered into nontribal marriage partnerships, marrying white men and claiming their own tribal rights status on the homelands, creating a so-called squaw man culture deeply resented by Indian males and traditionalists. The roles that women have played in creating these patterns—though of course men, too, found themselves in such circumstances—have not been examined very thoroughly in any comprehensive study that I know of, and there are suggestions that tribal experiences differ widely. This is a subject which no one wants to bring up, for it involves, quite obviously, a crucial matter of survival for societies which are said to be based upon the establishment of tribal bloodlines as survival mechanisms.

Preliminary work in anthropology, linguistics, native studies, or sociology must be continued in the next decades in order to find complete answers to questions concerning the role of modern women in modern Indian societies. The possibilities for the modern Indian woman in leadership roles, we may find, could be quite different in the future. Because of the development of the reservation-based community college system just prior to the 1970s, the emergence of several models of Native American Studies as an academic discipline at key universities and community colleges across the country, namely in South Dakota, Arizona, Minnesota, Washington, New Mexico, and California to name only a few sites, change is inevitable. It may no longer be a necessity nor a foregone conclusion that an Indian woman educated in the university system to eventually become a part of it will be required to abandon the traditions of her tribal culture in order to be successful in an academic professional life, either away from her homelands or on her reservation.

In contrast, it may be quite possible within the parameters of Indian Studies curricula to develop a professional life, to maintain a personal life among one's own people and other native groups, and to transcend the tyrannies of long-standing stereotypes brought about by or articulated through the either/or dichotomy of the past. The dynamics of an intellectual life deeply rooted in colonized intent may be diminished considerably in the next century. I'm sure that is the hope of native scholars across the land.

Indian woman will concede, however, that the stories of their lives, mostly written by white men, have not evolved very much in the Western imagination. They have been dismayed to see themselves portrayed in a mainstream movie called *A River Runs Through It*, as "easy," if nothing else—useful for the examination of the liberal conscience of the regional Montana male character.[2] There is much evidence that we have not moved on considerably from the Sacajewea model.

The other day I picked up a pamphlet which included a story about Indian women. It was published by the Bonanza publishing company of Bend, Oregon, and was written by Rick Steber, a writer whose work is unknown to me. The story is called "The Gold Pocket Watch," and it is reprinted here. Keep in mind that this is a contemporary telling; in other words, it is a continuing story. Some writer, perhaps Willa Cather, once said that there are only two or three human stories, and they keep getting retold. This is certainly true of the stories about Indian women in the West.

The young Siuslaw woman was on hand the day three white men came. She led them into her village. Council was called: the three men stood trial and it was judged they must die to atone for crimes committed by white men in the past. Their punishment was to be burned at the stake. Years later one of the men, a fellow named Summers, recalled the events that transpired:

> A young squaw, a pretty girl, came around and peered at me. It was with the greatest difficulty, for I was bound to a tree with a leather thong, that I was able to work my hand into my trouser pocket. I had a few trinkets and I dropped them onto the ground one at a time. She picked them up.
>
> I had nothing more to give. Then I hit upon the idea of enticing her with my pocket watch. I worked it free, held it by the chain and dangled it there in front of her eyes while telling her in Indian jargon that if she helped me escape, the pocket watch would be hers.
>
> She departed without the slightest hint she would come to my aid. But later, after dark, I felt someone cutting the thong that bound my hands. It was the girl. And after she had freed me, I cut loose my two companions. Before we escaped I kept my promise, giving my watch to the girl and promising her I would return one day.
>
> After I was safely away I never had cause to travel near the Indian village again, until years later. It was when I was about to ford the Umpqua River at the Reedsport Crossing that I happened to notice an Indian woman holding my gold pocket watch. She was the one who had saved me. And in the end I made this faithful woman my wife.

It is difficult for me to tell you how filled with disgust I am at this stereotypical and persistent story, but I must try. First of all, it suggests that, while the tribe has "laws" ("Council was called"), somehow, *women are exempt from tribal law*. How is it that the native woman, possessor of great power in the tribal community, symbol of honor and respect in religion, the core of kinship relation and commitment, can be so "easy," available and willing, in the eyes of the white man? Does she have no conscience? Is she ignorant? Is he so desired, so generous, so virtuous? The politics of this view, while scholars may dismiss this story itself as inferior and not a part of the literate discourse on the subject, cannot be mistaken.

Secondly, her "aiding and abetting" of the enemy goes unpunished and suggests, instead, that her status in the world, that is, her eventual marriage to the white man, is her reward. This kind of popular story about Indian women is said to be historical and legendary, illuminating at least one kind of relationship that the white man has wished to establish with the native peoples of this land through their women. On the other hand, it is the kind of story which attempts to structure a new reality for Indian women, one in which they have no responsibility, no role in a continuing tribal lifeway, and it becomes an allegory of her isolation from duty. She need not concern herself about the condition of her people.

William Bennett is quite right when he says that the teaching of literature is the teaching of values, of aesthetic and political order. The political message of these Western stories about Indian women is quite clear: the existence of a national life for Indians is dismissed by Indian woman who are dazzled by trinkets. Bennett is equally on target when he rails about canon theory and the development of literary criticism, because those are the control mechanisms for the discipline of literary and humanistic studies.

The fact is that there is a clear preference for the teaching of Native American literature courses in English departments on university campuses which has, in the last decade, overridden the interest in establishing political science and native language courses as the *core* development in Native American Studies as an academic discipline with departmental status. Perhaps because I come from an Indian world, in which the stories are held in high regard, I have wondered about this preference and have been concerned about the kind of stories which are studied. It was not very long ago that there was little or no distinction made between literature *about* Indians and literature *by* Indians. I have been curious, then, about the various strategies applied in English department course development. Part of the strategy to control the story has been to fail in permitting Indians and others to participate fully, for few faculty positions in American universities are held by natives, and there are even fewer Indian critics. Thus, the study of literary values, aesthetics and politics can become whatever the existing faculty wants it to become.

Movements in academia have recognized the need for change and have gained great momentum recently. Programs in Indian Studies, Feminist Studies, Chicano/a Studies, Black Studies, and Asian Studies are developments in academic disciplines which should allow appropriate defensive, regulatory, and transformative roles for the bodies of knowledge under consideration here. We must acknowledge how crucial it is to the future that these movements go forward.

I believe that it is possible to gain credibility for American Indian intellectual goals within a cultural and historical framework called Indian Studies (or Native American Studies, as it is called at some universities) rather than in the development of ancillary and multicultural ideas through already established disciplines and structures (i.e., literary studies, Sociology, and English Departments). Such a framework as Indian Studies as it has been envisioned in the last two or three decades may be one of the most crucial developments concerning the education of American Indians, both male and female, that can affect modern Indian life.

Indian Studies is a development which is dependent upon two parameters and, oddly enough, they have nothing to do with gender. The first is the religious, philosophical consideration of tribal life (culture), in which *worldview* is a major subject of inquiry; and the second is the legal and historical relationship of Indian Nations to the United States of America and other nations of the world (history), the essential principle of *sovereignty* being a primary focus of examination and definition. Because these parameters have been established over a very long period of time and because they are tribally specific, they do not operate as barriers to intellectual freedom; rather they operate as defensive, regulatory, and transformative guidelines that take into account rather than dismiss the experiences and values of our ancestors.

Essential to this model is the participation of Indians themselves as professors, researchers, and thinkers, and it is this criterion which distinguishes the discipline of Native Studies from anthropology, which is a science built on ideas of exogenous study as unbiased study. It is important that the parameters of the discipline be defined, examined, redefined, and reexamined according to the experiences of American Indians themselves and in the context of a shifting and developing body of knowledge. This is the nature of knowledge, of course; it is the nature of knowing and is essential to a developing intellectual perspective about the world.

American Indians can then examine the consequences of defining the parameters in a specific way, look at the consequences of the violation of the parameters, examine the points of conflict, and find solutions useful to their communities. They can assist in making decisions for their communities and tribes and will no longer be dependent upon bureaucrats in Washington, D. C., who pass laws which violate those parameters without studying the consequences. Life can become more stable on the homelands, and aggressive political legislation by representatives isolated from reality can be avoided, so that the extreme ups and downs with regard to economics and sovereignty can be tempered. Most importantly, the native scholar will not need to view the educational system as a hostile place and can become a full participant, not just a victim or complainer, in the discourse concerning this democracy's society and culture.

The tribal woman who is involved in the development of Indian Studies as an academic discipline is probably less likely to be polarized or isolated from tribal needs and aspirations. The model itself revitalizes, not only by permitting her to pursue the intellectual, philosophical, political, and social matters essential to the survival of her Indian nation, but by requiring that she undertake the responsibilities she rightfully acknowledges as hers.

Often Native American women in higher education or in disciplines other than Native Studies continue to exist outside the parameters of tribal life unless they are engaged in the development of the reservation-based university system. They have joined the mainstream of American intellectual life and have achieved success in a world with little or no connection to the legacies of tribal history. Their ambitions, focused upon assimilation rather than on the thoughtful consideration of what tribal nationalism means in the twenty-first century, have been their agony. Unless strict attention is paid to the structures of knowledge being developed in academia and unless Indian Studies as an academic discipline is taken seriously, the intellectual life of native women will continue to encounter coercive limitation rather than becoming a legitimate option.

10

The Big Pipe Case

"It is true," says an old Dakota legend, "that women have always had a very hard time. Their richness and joy is in having many children and numerous relatives."

What mainstream America may know about Sioux Indians is that they name Civil War captains "Dances with Wolves." What social scientists and politicians know stems from their relentless gathering of dismal statistics concerning poverty, alcoholism, early death, and fetal alcohol syndrome in tribal childbearing.[1] Probably one of the things that the American public most needs to know is that the enforced movement toward modernity for Indians is embedded in a legal world which can best be described as a confusing and vast folly emerging from the nineteenth-century Major Crimes Act, and that for no one has this folly been more profoundly dangerous than for the women of the tribes, who were, literally and figuratively, stripped of their authority in tribal life.

The modern attack on the civil and tribal rights of Indian women of childbearing age on reservation homelands suggests that life for them is not only "hard," as the legend says, but that modern change has often resulted in staggering, violent, misogynistic practices previously unknown to the tribes. As alcohol and native women have interacted with the imported legal system of the white man, the once-honored women of tribal societies have become scapegoats for the failed system. As the U. S. government has taken legal charge of Indian lives, the results of its work in a specific, exemplary case are worth contemplating.

In 1989, a grand jury issued an indictment of a teenage, alcoholic Indian mother in South Dakota who, denied abortion services, gave birth to her third infant. It was charged that the Indian mother neglected and "assaulted her with intent to commit serious bodily injury" by breast-feeding the infant while under the influence, thereby committing a felony.[2]

The court, without a jury trial, sentenced her to almost four years in a federal penitentiary at Lexington, Kentucky. Shortly thereafter, the tribal court terminated her parental rights to this child and two previous children. The court believes it has "done the right thing."

"Do not forget," admonished the U. S. Attorney for South Dakota at that time, Philip Hogen, "a lot of caring people got involved. They investigated the conditions in the home. They went to the authorities and they got that child out of there and she is now in foster care. And Sadie Big Pipe (not her real name) who will soon be two years old, is going to live. . . . I hope that you are not going to forget that there were courageous, caring people involved here, and that they did exactly the right thing."

The early details of the entire episode might, for some, seem to bear out Mr. Hogen's position. When tribal police were called to the Big Pipe home at Lower Brule that spring day, they saw a nearly starved infant and a drunken mother. They went to the tribal judge and, with the help of social workers, the Community Health Representative (CHR) and others removed the nursing child from the home and took her to the only hospital in the area, some twenty miles off the reservation in Chamberlain, South Dakota.

The child had a bad diaper rash, virus-caused ulcers on her legs, and an alcohol level in her blood measured at .02. The infant, then nine weeks old, weighed 5 pounds and 4 ounces. While no infant should ever ingest alcohol, many medical assessments of this level suggest that it is, perhaps, not in every case "medically consequential."

The mother's blood-alcohol levels, on the other hand, measured at different intervals over the next two weeks as she was incarcerated and released, were .10, .12, and .30 (.10 being legally intoxicated and unable to drive a car). These levels suggest that the mother's condition was worsening, and many medical persons believe them to be dangerous. Some say that at a level of .25 some people lose consciousness, and at .50 death may occur. Yet, Marie Big Pipe was never hospitalized, nor was she sent to a detoxification center during this entire episode.

Within days, the South Dakota State Department of Social Services took custody of the child. The action was called a "rescue" in formal reports. Because Marie Big Pipe was indigent, the federal courts appointed an attorney for her and then released her on condition that she "refrain from the use of alcohol" and "enroll in an out-patient alcohol treatment center." Ten days later, the court revoked the release when Marie was arrested on charges of intoxication in violation of the bond.

Another ten days passed before a hearing was scheduled, during which time the court stated that the teenaged mother "[had] a serious history of alcohol abuse and [was] unable to control her use of alcohol without an inpatient treatment program; that currently there [were] no inpatient facilities capable of providing placement; and that she [was] unlikely to abide by any terms and conditions of release to assure her court appearance." The court ordered that she be held in custody and that a jury trial be scheduled for two weeks later.

Marie's attorney from Chamberlain, the second lawyer on the case, who was appointed by the court when the previously appointed lawyer from Gregory, several hours' drive away from the reservation, withdrew, filed a futile motion to dismiss. His argument was that the heart of the matter was the legal definition of "assault with intent to commit serious bodily injury" as only involving beatings and did not apply to nursing babies and their alcoholic mothers. Basically, he said, the issue was whether her actions constituted "neglect," a misdemeanor; or assault with "intent" to commit serious bodily injury," a felony.

Black's Law Dictionary defines assault as "any willful attempt or threat to inflict injury upon the person of another when coupled with an apparent present ability to do so, and any intentional display of force such as would give the victim reason to fear or expect immediate bodily harm . . . an assault may be committed without actually touching, or striking, or doing bodily harm, to the person of another." Neglect, as defined in *Black's*, "may mean to omit, fail or forbear to do a thing which can be done, but it may also import an absence of care or attention in the doing or omission of a given act. And it may mean a designed refusal or unwillingness to perform one's duty."

The U. S. Attorney in his opposition to the motion to dismiss argued that Marie's "decision not to care for the baby is an intentional act of omission which is sufficient under the circumstances of this case to constitute an assault." He went on to say that "her act of giving the infant alcoholic beverages or allowing alcohol to enter the baby's system is sufficient to constitute an assault against the child." The motion to dismiss was denied. Marie's health problems were criminalized, her parental actions defined as crimes, and her family forever destroyed.

A jury was never impaneled, and five months later a federal judge quietly sent Marie Big Pipe to the Kentucky prison for nearly four years. There was no outcry—not from the attorney who handled her case, nor from the Indian community of relatives and friends, nor from Marie herself.

Twisted History Declares Women a Threat

The principal effects of overt federal legal action to condemn Indian parenthood and take Indian children away from Indian parents have been the subject of controversy in native communities for a century, during which time Indian children were routinely snatched from dysfunctional tribal families by state agencies and other concerned parties. Finally, in defense of themselves, the tribes fought for the 1978 Indian Child Welfare Act, saw it passed, and convinced themselves that help was on its way. The irony of the usurpation of this legislation in specific cases such as Marie Big Pipe's is a cruel one. No matter what the tribes assert in theory, they are faced with a paternalizing federal mandate.

One of the convincing arguments against criminalizing an Indian parent's action and terminating forever the rights of recalcitrant parents was articulated in the mid-1970s by Ramona Bennett, chairwoman of the Puyallup Tribe of Washington State:

The alienations of Indian children from their parents can become a serious mental health problem. If you lose your child you are dead; you are never going to get rehabilitated or you are never going to get well. If there are problems, once the children are gone, the whole family unit is never going to get well.

If this is true, who will help Marie Big Pipe get well? If she does not get well, what is the future for any of us?

To suggest that an ill parent (an alcoholic parent) should be made a criminal and that her children should be forever removed from her presence, violates one of the principles of Chairwoman Bennett's brilliant and useful discussion, twenty years ago, on the welfare of Indian children. The effort to get tribal jurisdiction over tribal children was not made so that objectionable parents, particularly mothers, could forever be banished from tribal life through criminalization and incarceration.

Every Indian parent will tell you that the welfare of tribal children is dependent upon the welfare of tribal parents, not the state or federal government. Foster care, placement, termination of parental rights, preadoptive placement, and adoptive placement, while now in the hands of the tribal officials since the passage of Indian Child Welfare Act in 1978, were never meant to become instruments destructive to families. How has this all happened? Why? Who is responsible?

A Little Background

From about 1944 through 1964, the United States government, using its powers of eminent domain, seized thousands of acres of Lakota/Dakota, treaty-protected reservation lands in the northern plains to bring domestic electricity and agricultural irrigation to the region. In the process, Indian communities (including the Lower Brule reservation, which is the home of Marie Big Pipe and her relatives) were destroyed by flooding. As if nothing could stop the mid-century rush for hydropower, communities of the Missouri River tribes of the Sioux were uprooted and moved, and it has taken decades to even begin to heal the wounds. Traditional governing groups steeped in long-sustained cultural values were fragmented, economic systems and reservation infrastructures were destroyed, as they had been in the late 1800s. Churches, cemeteries, governmental, medical, and educational facilities were flooded out, moved out, and never replaced.

The South Dakota Indian reservations called Crow Creek and Lower Brule, across the river from each other, the smallest groups of the Sioux Nation and the setting for events in this article, were particularly devastated. As the physical landscape was torn apart, so was the fabric of the social and cultural life of the tribes. *Termination* was the word which described the federal policy toward these communities and these people.

Accompanying the physical devastation on the reservations was the backlash of paternalism, racism, and mysogyny by the nearby white populations and the federal government, which now claimed supremacy and domination over these reservation lands and resources. Decades later, the Sioux Nation and most other native communities are still fighting an undeclared war for their sovereign rights against an ineffectual and stifling paternalistic bureaucracy. And Sioux women, exemplars of their own tribal histories, are subjected to an incapacitating colonial tyranny.

There is evidence that women, thought by the tribes to be the backbone of native society and the bearers of sacred children and repositors of cultural values, are now thought to pose a significant threat to tribal survival. Indeed, the intrusive federal government now interprets the law on Indian reservations in ways which sanction indicting alcoholic, childbearing Indian woman as though they alone are responsible for the fragmentation of the social fabric of Indian lives. As infants with fetal alcohol syndrome (FAS) and fetal alcohol effect (FAE) are born in increasing numbers, it is said that womens' recalcitrant behavior (consuming alcohol and other drugs during pregnancy and nursing) needs to be legally criminalized by the federal system to make it a felony for a woman to commit such acts.

The collaboration of tribal, federal, and state law-enforcement agencies in recent times, particularly, has done little to support Indian values or put any value on the Indian family. In fact, many Indian women's groups believe it does the opposite by solidifying non-Indian values and perpetuating the separation of family. What the imposed laws have finally done is to declare that what used to be a tribal societal problem, that is, a failure to protect women and children from harm, is now solely a woman's failure, a woman's despair, a woman's fault, a woman's crime. Young Indian women, many with minimal education and weakened familial support systems, have been subjected to closer scrutiny by social services and the court system than ever before. They have become objects of scorn, singled out for a particular kind of punishment dictated by their alcoholism, drug use, and promiscuity. They are seen as a root cause of the rise in infant mortality, abuse, and fetal deformity.

The white man's law and the tribe's adoption of Anglo government have removed the traditional forms of punishment and control for criminal acts. As tribal police, court systems, state social service agencies, and Christian conservatives replace traditional tribal ideas and systems of control, the legal focus on the young, childbearing Indian woman as culprit and criminal has been of major concern to women's groups.

In prior days, while childbearing was considered women's business, it was not thought to be separated from the natural and ethical responsibilites of males. Therefore, men who caused stress in the community or risk to the survival of the tribe by dishonoring women were held accountable by the people. They could not carry the sacred pipe, nor could they hold positions of status. They were often physically attacked by the woman's male relatives and driven from tribal life. These particular controls in tribal society often no longer apply. In many tribal communities, such men who are known to degrade women and abandon children, now hold positions of power, even sometimes sitting at the tribal council tables. They are directors of tribal programs, and they often participate unmolested in sacred ceremonies. Many others who may not purposefully or intentionally degrade women often remain silent about the atrocities and hypocrisies they see in their communities. In the process of their public lives they assist in transferring to women the responsibility for the social ills of the tribes.

Such contradictions may occur, some suggest, because the historical influence of Christian religions and Anglo law in native communities has made it possible for individuals to abandon long-held views concerning marriage patterns and tribal arrangements for childbearing and parental responsibilties. Interracial marriages and illicit sexual relationships, denied the sanction of the tribes and families, often ignore the particular responsibilities prescribed for both males and females in traditional societies. Failures in these duties were dealt swift and severe punishment, but seldom was male honor in matters of marriage and sex abandoned as routinely as it is today. Young women, while held accountable for their actions, were seldom the only ones condemned in matters of this kind, as they are today.

If the Marie Big Pipe case is any indication of law enforcement and justice on the reservation, it is a sad portrayal of the failure of the system and the subsequent loss of a woman's human and civil rights, and obviously of her treaty rights as well. The complex issue of Indian sovereignty, that is, the "power of self-governance and the inherent right to control their internal affairs," while beyond the scope of this article, is as much a subject of this discussion as is a woman's right to protection by the law.

Federal Authority Criminalizes the Disease of Alcoholism

In South Dakota two sovereign entities have criminal jurisdiction over crimes commited on reservations: the Indian nation and the federal government. Who has jurisdiction depends on various factors, such as the severity or degree of the crime, the location, who committed the crime, and against whom.

Indian jurisdiction has been steadily eroded by Congress through the Major Crimes Act (18 U.S.C. 1153), which transferred jurisdiction over major crimes committed on reservations to the federal government. This act was passed by Congress in 1885 as a result of public reaction to the Supreme Court's holding that federal courts lacked jurisdiction over a Sioux Indian who had already been punished by his tribe (the Sicangu) for the killing of another Indian (the now famous ex-parte Crow Dog case). The Act is now seen by many as a major incursion into traditional tribal powers.

Fourteen enumerated crimes (originally there were only seven) are now under the provision of this federal jurisdiction. The charge of assault, the definition of which has been broadened and redefined through the appeals process, is now used by the courts and social agencies on reservations to redefine a woman's health issues in terms of criminal behavior.

If such federal litigation as has been allowed in the Big Pipe case occurs because of the federal govenment's notion of its own superiority, it may also be the function of a deep-seated mysogyny that white feminists say is at the core of American society. In either case, it pits mother against child in a way that is unbearable to thinking American Indians. Yet, almost everybody is too stunned by the rising statistics of bitter violence in Indian communities, substance abuse, divorce, family violence, murder, crimes of brother against brother, cruelty toward women and the elderly, child abuse and neglect, and wife-beating, to defy the idea that making criminals out of young, childbearing Indian women and applying for federal funds to build "shelters" are viable solutions.

In such an outrageously dangerous world, it is thought, there has to be someone to blame. Quickly, easily, thoughtlessly, the blame is directed toward a defenseless victim who is said to be victimizing others, and Marie Big Pipe becomes everyone's target. This is nothing new in America, known for its culture of quick and easy solutions, but it is something new to many Indians whose societies have often cherished the idea that for the weak, the young, the aged, ill and orphaned, there has been a special tribal care-taking obligation.

Indian America knows that Marie Big Pipe, ill and weak, too young to help herself, was neither to blame nor blameless. More than any-thing, Indian America knows that *she, too, is its daughter, neither criminal nor saint.*

The Big Pipe case is one of thousands in America today, many of which occur on reservations, that represents an outrageous violation of human rights for those who come from tribal societies in which the child is a sacred gift and motherhood a cultural ideal, to be protected as the quintessential survival mechanism of an ethical society. It makes a mockery of the 1948 Universal Declaration of Human Rights which states that "Motherhood and Childhood (not just childhood) are entitled to special care and assistance."

America Defends Itself against Marie Big Pipe

It is interesting to note that U. S. federal attorneys have discretion in which cases they will try, that they pick and choose the cases which will justify their time and purpose. It is probably no accident that federal authorities, with either the acquiescence of or a directive from tribal authorities, decided upon the criminality of Marie Big Pipe's actions for reasons well articulated in the early findings. The child abuse or neglect charge could have been brought by the tribal authorities, because it is still within their jurisdiction to prosecute misdemeanor charges, but it was rejected in favor of the federal "assault resulting in serious bodily harm" charge available from the federal arsenal of legal remedies.

This decision-making process probably deserves further discussion, which should center upon whether the law provides appropriate remedy to Indian communities beset with poverty, social ills, inadequate education, health, housing, and legal facilities, to say nothing of constant harrassment concerning jurisdictional issues from federal, state, and county governments. (In South Dakota, the tribes confront steady efforts by the courts to overturn settled law in everything from hunting to casino gaming issues, often with the blessing of the state and federal legislators.)

For whom should the law provide extraordinary protection under these particular conditions, and what is the role to be played by the courts? Unfortunately, tribal courts have no jurisdiction over many offenses committed on their homelands. Even when they do have jurisdictional decisions to make, however, they often fail to rise to the occasion.

In the Big Pipe case, former U. S. Attorney Phil Hogen says, "There is no ideal federal statute for this kind of offense or crime of omission, though it was, of course, a classic case of child abuse/neglect. The assault resulting in serious bodily injury is the charge that most nearly fit."

Most nearly fit? This is a clear failure of the courts and the lawyers in Indian Country to take to a jury not only a challenge to the feminization of the "assault" charge which some believe has been the result of more than a decade of conservative, right-wing thinking, but also a challenge to any argument over whether alcoholism is a crime or a disease. If alcoholism is a disease rather than a crime, as defined by the federal government (and by the American Medical Association since 1956), why didn't this case reflect that description? While there is no question Marie's infant was not receiving love and care and nourishment from her mother, whose responsibility it was to see that she came to no harm, there is no evidence that this neglectful, ill, addicted mother could be described as incorrigible, nor genetically defective, evil, vengeful, nor criminally violent for the purpose of domination or control, nor any of the other more egregious or radical definitions of criminality. Even a doctor's deposition, presented in her defense, indicated that there was no evidence of "malicious, evil intent" on her part.

The Indian Public Health facility, the institution in charge of health care for her people, and to which she turned for help, provides some assistance in birth control but denies access to abortion services and probably fails in its counseling of young women of childbearing age. At this time, there is little or no sex education in most federal and tribal schools.

Needless to say, the oppressive Christian religious presences on reservations, the churches, the schools (which exert considerable influence in Indian communities), the dismissal of traditional native female guidance and medical advice by existing, reservation-based institutions—all these combined to stifle Marie Big Pipe's natural inclination to do what she knew was best for her in this instance.

Drinking heavily at the time, depressed, apathetic, and in serious ill health, she knew she wanted an abortion but did not have the confidence, the personal knowledge, nor the financial means to seek out abortion services on her own. Medical practitioners know that when a woman's *choice* to bear children is removed in cases like this, suicide can be the next logical step. Alcohol may have been Marie's method of suicide or, at the very least, self-obliteration if one wants to make a case for willful behavior. Abortion services, including counseling on options, are legally outlawed in reservation hospitals, and there are no hospital facilities at all on the Crow Creek and Lower Brule Sioux reservations, an area of several hundred thousand acres.

There is only one abortion clinic in South Dakota, located in Sioux Falls, several hours' drive from the Lower Brule reservation. Its physician, Dr. Buck Williams, OB/GYN, has appeared on national television saying he fears for his life as the result of threats from antiabortion factions in the state. Dr. Williams says he wears a bulletproof vest and carries a gun. Pro-lifers in the state have threatened to "cut off my fingers," he has said.

Interviews with Marie reveal a troubled young woman burdened by inadequate education and unable to make choices (her schooling at a local Catholic boarding school was ended at seventh grade). Her mention of the sexual abuse and repeated rapes she endured over a long period of her young life at home and at the boarding school were never taken seriously by any of her mostly male interviewers.

Not taking any of these matters under advisement, handling the case as though it were without context, failing to take the responsibility to alleviate the suffering of both victims in this case, the United States' denial of the motion to dismiss argued that Marie Big Pipe's "decision not to care for the baby was an intentional act of omission, which is sufficient under the circumstances of this case to constitute an assault. Furthermore, her act of giving the infant alcoholic beverages or allowing alcohol to enter the baby's system is sufficient to constitute an assault against the child."

It argued further that Marie's actions "were more than neglect. She intentionally decided to starve the child so that she would not be around to further 'mess up her life.' "

This argument was based upon a narrative written by a white male agent of the FBI who interrogated her months after she was arrested. This interview, conducted in the presence of a white female social worker from the South Dakota Department of Social Services in Pierre, was in the eyes of the judge particularly damning. The FBI agent wrote,

Big Pipe stated that she felt that Sadie was the source of all her problems. She did not want to have her and tried everything she could think of to induce an abortion while she was carrying her. She continued to drink all during the pregnancy, she would do situps, and jump up and down in an effort to induce an abortion. She even investigated having a surgical abortion performed but was unable to find any agency that would pay for it so she did not have it done. She still wanted to have an abortion performed on herself after the three-month limit but could find no one to help or to pay for it. She felt that the pregnancy "screwed up" her good life with her new boyfriend. He would not accept the pregnancy or the baby since it would not be his. Even after the baby was born, she didn't want it and could barely bring herself to touch it or care for it. It made her mad and angry because she had "messed up [her] life." Her older daughter didn't like her either and did not want her around. Marie cares a great deal for this older daughter's feelings and felt bad for her being against the baby but understood how she felt, she had ruined her life, too.

The government, in its prosecution of Marie Big Pipe, referred to a newspaper article from July, 1989, which reported a mother in New York who abandoned her baby in the woods and was charged with first-degree assault and first-degree reckless endangerment. The government pressed this parallel, though its speciousness was readily apparent since Marie had not abandoned her baby. Indeed, Marie said she tried not to nurse the infant while she was under the influence of alcohol but the infant refused to take the bottle with its prepared formula. Because a jury was not impaneled to hear the discussion of all relevant inquiry, and the question of "intent" was never fully explored, the case clearly was stacked against the defendant.

By the end of five months of local incarceration, Marie's will to continue her "not guilty" stance had worn down completely. She

finally signed a statement which her lawyer claims she had written
and understood:

My attorney has explained my . . . rights . . . and explained the facts of this
incident and what impact they will have upon a jury. He also explained that
whether I assaulted my daughter by neglecting her is a unique case and presents
a fairly significant factual issue for the jury. Even if [sic] would lose this case by
a jury verdict, the issue of assault by neglect presents a strong appealable issue.

My attorney has further explained that this will not be an easy case to win,
because of the emotional impact of a malnourished child.

I have decided to plead guilty to the charge lodged against me. I do so with
the understanding that I waive my right to appeal the issue of assault/neglect
and all other constitutional rights I have. I chose to plead guilty because of the
possibility of a jury conviction, the trauma of a jury trial, and the desire to avoid
having this entire matter aired to the court.

In subsequent writings that seem particularly poignant and naive,
Marie said her counsel "would urge that any sentence I receive will
be served in the Springfield Correction Institution in Springfield, South
Dakota." She also said that she wanted to get her baby back and take
care of her. The honorable Chief Judge of the U. S. District Court,
Donald J. Porter, would have none of it, of course, and sentenced her to
"hard time."

Marie Big Pipe is home now, after more than two years in a federal
prison. She is on probation until 1996. Her grandmother says, "She done
her time and she just wants to put it behind her." Many people connected
with the case refuse to discuss it publicly.

Damaged Tribal Families

One of the pragmatic realities for contemporary Indians in the defense
of themselves is that, too often, lawyers who are supposedly defending
them on their homelands, overwhelmed with the complexity surround-
ing issues of jurisdiction and structure, just "carry the brief," or plea
bargain the cases before them. These lawyers rarely vigorously defend
their clients by establishing precedents which might prove useful to
the development of a civilized legal system on Indian homelands in
America.

By simply plea bargaining in this case, Marie Big Pipe's lawyer failed
to persuade her that they should proceed with a jury trial, or look at
the legal issues this case presented. He says he responded in accordance
with "his client's wishes" and did not take it to a jury because, he says,
his client was reluctant to have the matter aired before the jury.

This rationale seems unconvincing, since we have here a woman with a minimal education who relied on her attorney. He should have taken this case to the jury and called for a reassessment of the new legal definitions by which the illnesses of Indian women and their loss of human and reproductive rights continue to be criminalized. As is generally true of Indians with court-appointed attorneys, Marie just didn't get good legal advice. Her quick and painful legal history, then, and the inglorious and corrupt history of the white man's law as it has been applied to indigenous peoples, are inextricably tied.

In the sense that justice is rarely separated from political and legislative processes, neither is it separate from the national ideologies which are expressed therein. Today's politics of the war upon women everywhere (I refer you not only to older works like Brownmiller's *Against Our Wills*, but also the new work on the Hill/Thomas case, *Strange Justice*) and the suppression of Indian women's rights—reproductive rights in particular—is not unconnected to the suppression of the rights of the indigenes historically. The historical fear that federal power will somehow suffer and that America will suffer damage if tribal government and courts reflect tribal cultural ideals which suggest that *Lakota womanhood is sacred* seems to prevail.

Law is not beyond context, and no one can ignore the effects of historical oppression. Some believe it all seemed to happen quickly and inadvertently. In 1885, a rider to an Indian General Appropriations Act, which seemed to some to be just an unimportant paragraph, soon became the basis for the oppressive Major Crimes Act mentioned earlier in this article. My view of it all is much more cynical because of the consequences. This quick and inadvertent action divested the tribes of virtually any legal and moral jurisdiction over their lives, and it was the beginning of a fearsome justice on Indian lands. It became the law's answer to the political questions posed by "vanishing American" theories resulting in assimilation and genocide. It became the major political tool used in the destruction of long-standing, humane Native American ethical and legal systems.

It is argued by some Native American scholars that the responsibilities inherent in ethical childbearing issues were always in the hands of women, never in legal nor in male societies. Today, on Indian reservations, you can find women's organizations fighting to regain the reproductive rights that they say were once theirs in sympathetic and comforting tribal societies. Responsible men and women of the tribes are working toward developing culturally based systems through which their social lives may be improved. Their antagonists, however, the paternalistically driven federal institutions which have for so long fought for power over tribal infrastructures, are still in place.

The principal effect of the nineteenth-century, white-male-sponsored Major Crimes Act was to permit prosecution of Indians by reference to selected federal criminal statutes applicable on federal reservations. Seven crimes were originally covered. To make sure that no illegal acts escaped punishment, however, the U. S. Congress, only four years after assuming that jurisdiction, passed the Assimilative Crimes Act in 1889, which allowed the government to take on cases for the states. This act includes the following language:

Whoever is guilty of an act or omission which although not made punishable by any enactment of Congress, would be punishable if committed or omitted within the jurisdiction of State, Territory, Possession, or District in which such place is situated . . . shall be guilty of a like offense and subject to a like punishment.

What this has meant in Indian country is that when local, state, and regional laws cannot apply, the federal government can "assimilate" them, in other words, assume control, and this often results in making state criminal laws applicable on Indian land, in violation of cultural belief systems or anything else. It is, perhaps, redundant to say that all of this congressional activity was undertaken in violation of the 1868 treaty between the Sioux Nation and the United States, which defends as one its principles the upholding of tribal sovereignty.

By a series of amendments, then, and through case law, the former list of seven major crimes has been expanded to the present fourteen: murder, manslaughter, kidnapping, rape, carnal knowledge by a man of any female not his wife or sixteen years of age, assault with the intent to commit rape, incest, assault with the intent to commit murder, assault with a dangerous weapon, assault resulting in serious bodily harm, arson, burglary, robbery, and larceny.

All of these crimes have been removed over the years from tribal jurisdiction by white American politicians and lawyers, the U. S. Congress, and the courts. These imponderable forces have often conspired with malice aforethought, in my view, to colonize and suppress a sovereign nation of people, and even now, with this distortion of American democracy exposed, everyone, lawyers and victims alike, continues to turn away.

The expanded definitions of *assault, abuse,* and *neglect* are used now to punish childbearing Indian women suffering from alcoholism as a result of that historical jurisdictional *fait accompli* before the turn of the century when Indians had absolutely no access to the U. S. courts.

In spite of these new definitions, which must be deplored, there is still the question of a jury trial. What happened to the idea of "a jury of your peers" as a facet of justice on Indian reservations? In the Big Pipe case, held in the Ninth District, a jury trial might have made a difference not only for Marie but for all of us. In one of its lucid moments in 1973 the Supreme Court rendered a decision (*Keeble v. United States*, 412 USA 204) which said that an Indian is entitled to an *instruction on a lesser included offense* because he or she is entitled to be tried "in the same manner" as a non-Indian under 18 USCA x 3242. While this is not a perfect solution to sovereignty issues, an argument to a jury of her "peers" might have been convincing and might have given the courts a chance to make distinctions between criminal actions and health issues. This maneuver might have put matters back in community hands where native belief systems could have been a part of the solution mechanism. Without the protection of a jury trial, a judge (*always* white and male in South Dakota) may simply refuse to consider other objections and responses.

If Marie had been tried and convicted of "simple assault," she would have been subject to a $500 fine and six months in tribal jail. Under other, more humane, systems of justice, she might even have undergone extensive medical treatment. She might have been appropriately assisted toward rehabilitation, and her family might have remained intact, her parental rights sustained. Tribal courts are, today, taking these matters under legal discussion, suggesting that the usurpation of tribal court authority in these cases is unconstitutional and that the infusion of massive federal funds into the tribal court systems for training and education would strengthen the integrity of their own communities.

Even with a jury trial, however, as juries are now constituted, there is no assurance that Marie would have been treated fairly. It appears that Indians in positions of power on reservations (mostly male) are themselves Christian religious leaders holding rigid, fundamentalist views, or they are police and social workers trained to defend the status quo, educated in the long-standing and destructive theories of race and law perpetuated in American educational systems. They often "go with the flow," say the lawyers and others who deal with these juries and tribal power systems. They vote with the majority when they vote. They often, as do most Americans, and midwesterners in general, have simplistic attitudes toward complex social and legal problems. Be that as it may, the impact of removing moral and legal jurisdiction from tribal control and placing it in the hands of "exterior," or "white men's," legal and legislative systems has been a disaster.

Most Indian individuals caught up in criminal charges learn that the legal system to which they are subjected is illogical, inconsistent, counterproductive and, often, anti-Indian and racist. Speeding or driving under the influence of alcohol on the reservation roads, for example, may get you arrested by the tribal police, or the state patrol, or a county sheriff, or no one at all, depending upon which of the latest jurisdictional battles has been won or lost. But one thing can be predicted: If you are a childbearing Indian woman, you will merit the special attention of the federal court system.

In fantasies of a perfect world, idealized models exist in which justice never fails, and people always get what they deserve. The reality is that for all of us in this world, and for American Indians in particular, there is a complex mixture of social, political, institutional, experiential, and personal factors from which courts pick and choose, lawyers argue, and judges rule.

There is, clearly, much work to be done by both whites and Indians before justice can prevail. Only one thing, say tribal leaders, scholars, and politicians, can rid Indians of this chaotic and destructive legal situation: a clear recognition of the sovereign nature of America's Indian nations—which means, in practical terms, land reform, cultural revitalization, and the legal, financial, educational, and economic control of our own resources. Most of all, it means the reform of a colonial system of law long despised by the people. The U. S. Congress, its president, and its courts are beginning to understand the need for true home rule on Indian lands, but no one should believe that the antagonists aren't still in place.

Part Five

THE LAST WORD

Part Five

The Last Word

I end this volume of essays in the same way I began it, by reading and commenting. This last part includes three commentaries which are personal and exploratory. It is my way of trying to have the last word, trying to point the way, and trying to say that it is perhaps inevitable that some of us wish to possess a conscience of solitariness and individuality, even though it may seem more and more uncherished in a loquacious world that is moving too quickly.

No matter what happens in modern America, you know, nontribal people always think they have the last word. They are the ones, they think, who are in charge of time and history. In rejection of that idea, I'm reminded of the story we Dakotas tell about the mountain just a few miles from my home that "they" are blowing up in the name of the famed Oglala Chieftain Crazy Horse. It is a desecration, of course, evidence of the utter arrogance of whites coming into these lands. Beyond that, though, it's a way for whites to tell themselves they will have the last word. We've made a joke of it now.

Keyapi: On the mountain, Crazy Horse is pointing to a place "over there, where my dead lie buried," in response to the white man sculptor's question: "Where are your homelands?"

Just then the white man made a mistake. He set his dynamite under the pointing finger of Crazy Horse and, accidentally, he blew the finger clean off. Now, in response to the question, Crazy Horse simply lifts his chin and points with his lips.

11

How Scholarship Comes to Be Relevant, or Dumbarton Oaks Is Fifty Years Old

Where I was born and lived until adulthood, about fifteen miles from Fort Thompson, South Dakota, on the Crow Creek Sioux Indian Reservation, there was not one public library, not even a reading collection in the little day school where I went to learn to read and write English. That's astonishing, I suppose, since the Indian reservation of which I speak has an area of over 285,930 acres, as large as many metropolitan areas you can name.

This was Buffalo County in the late thirties and early forties, a place and time of great poverty, I am told, though I didn't really know it then. We lived a warm, communal life with many relatives. My mother and my grandfather took turns taking me, my siblings, and whatever cousins we could round up to Chamberlain every now and then, to that white man's town that sits dumbly along the Missouri River. We could check out books there from a small, stuffy room on the second floor of the City Hall, just upstairs from the city jail which often housed one of my drinking uncles. There were some two hundred volumes there, but it could hardly have been called a library in the same way the city jail could hardly be called a place for the hard core.

Indians in those days sometimes got a letter from a Father at the reservation-based Catholic Mission when we went to those white-man towns, letters that said we were either reliable or we were not. In this case, Father D. said we could be trusted to return the books. We presented the letter to the city librarian, who gave us the impression that, in spite of the Father's commendation, we really needed to be watched carefully.

What this artless activity might mean, in part, is that those of us whose Indian parents, grandparents, and great-grandparents lived along the Crow Creek in those times learned early on to approach an alien and hostile world—an *other* world which exists in history and academia for the benefit of the literati, or the wealthy, or the urbane, or whomever we were not—cautiously and tentatively. The truth is that, as Indian reservation kids, we were probably not very interested in that world at all, and it is only in retrospect, as one who grew up to be a teacher, that I find the subject worth taking up.

You will just have to take my word for it that we who grew up differently, listening to the epic-filled Lakota/Dakota language of our people, hearing on the radio the high-pitched voice of Franklin D. Roosevelt about the New Deal as though it mattered to us, almost never get the message of how important and intimate that "other world," that "alien" world claims to be. It takes us years to find that out!

This is true, perhaps, because of what may be called a cultural gap. Or, it may be that it is true because of plain old poverty. Or, in our case in the northern plains, it may be caused by isolation which, in turn, may be the result of an acrimonious history that whites and Indians in the region share. Indeed, I think we as people of reservation lands were and probably are not very different in that regard from the people who live in thousands of rural enclaves in America then or now. Whatever the reasons, we had some vague notion, even then, that we were suffering during important years what may be called "library/book deprivation," which impeded our participation in the scholarly world. We knew then, I suppose, that our pathetic library treks were attempts at dealing with that deprivation. As I look back on it now, I know that my mother and my grandfather were on the right track.

Since most of the people I know do not end up attending Harvard University, and rarely do we read at the London Museum or Oxford, join fraternities or sororities at Dartmouth or Brown, travel to Europe as scholars, or meet ambassadors and prime ministers, we have only our own intellectual curiosity to assist us in knowing about that other world. Many of us have done all we can to catch up. To be honest, though, without a quality education there is always the feeling that one is blindly groping, fearful of what is to come because one must shed one's skin in order to become a newer version of the self. It's like the reptile who "becomes" by shedding his epidermis in the hot wind of a Dakota August. It is slow and agonizing. It is not unheard of for the asp to succumb to the constrictions in the process.

All of this was never more clear to me than when I walked past the Dumbarton Oaks estate in Georgetown a few years ago. Dumbarton Oaks, if it is not too obvious to say so, is a garden oasis of sixteen acres. And it is a library! One of a traditional sort. The name, as I walked past, was familiar to me only because I had read in some history text as an undergraduate that it was the place where Secretary of State Cordell Hull met with leaders from all over the world and the Soviet Union and China in that year of destiny, 1944, as a prelude to the formation of the United Nations. Somehow, I recalled the name Dumbarton Oaks from ancient memory banks as a name which had appeared on an exam I once took on the development of civilization. As I stared, the name lingered vaguely, and I knew I had miraculously committed something about it to memory. Ah! Description: "Research Library, emphasis Byzantine history."

I was on the far side of fifty and Dumbarton Oaks was nearly so as I walked along the sidewalk that April day. The place seemed so . . . ordinary. Could this be that historical edifice?

Spring snows had just recently melted from the grounds of the Dumbarton Oaks estate. Nothing had been cleaned up from a hard winter, and the whole place looked a bit shabby, dark, and unkempt. What was left of magnolias and autumn chrysanthemums cluttered the sidewalks and alcoves. A bronze plaque said that a world diplomat named Bliss had given the place to Harvard University as a repository of history and culture in order to "inform the future with wisdom." I walked up to the dull windows, shaded my eyes with my hands, and peered into the rooms filled with what looked like heavy, old, European furniture and Oriental rugs.

Was there no one about? I tried several doors as I walked around the buildings, but they were all locked. There was a white card stuck inside the door that said something about a showing of a pre-Columbian art collection, but there was no information concerning the hours and days of viewing. I strolled around the rumpled grounds and saw what I thought to be a greenhouse; even further on were smaller houses, newer brick ones. Huge, ancient oak trees, their leaves just starting to bud, were everywhere.

It occurred to me that this was, indeed, the historical Dumbarton Oaks, that its rooms held a collection of some thousands of volumes on Byzantine art, music, and ideas (later someone said 107,623); that hundreds of scholars from all over the world come here to study, that great concerts are held here, and important meetings go on all the time, like the one between the Marquis de Lafayette and Secretary of War

John C. Calhoun in 1824. All of this activity is carefully scheduled and monitored in the name of an empire which fell, some say, in 1453, a few decades prior to the voyage of Columbus to the so-called New World.

I stood still at the estate grounds that day. At first glance, it all seemed so irrelevant, and the joy I felt at putting together a name and a place and a memory from my exam quickly faded. But, no, I thought. It is not irrelevant. As an American Indian I understand the stroke of fate by which one civilization falls and another rises. At some level, all Indians, and indigenes everywhere, understand the issues of conquest, the death of nations, and the unexpected survival of ideas. And, surely, we Indians have spent enough time studying Europe and Asia in academia, to the exclusion of our own histories, distinguishing between the ideals of the Western world and its adversaries, speculating about how its great political, religious, and artistic dramas rose from what is referred to in the scholarly world as "paganism," to be fascinated about the process by which humans find answers about the universe. We, too, have resolved mysteries; we, too, know something about universal truths.

It also occurred to me that day that I might not be the only one who may have wanted to know more about the unspoken history of this place, this "other" place. Dumbarton Oaks, I found out later, was originally a plantation of the Old South where African slaves were kept for over two hundred years while white Americans were claiming they didn't know it was wrong or immoral. Even now it stands as a magnificent, legendary old castle of the American elite, still justifying itself and the absurd notion that all white men are "created equal." It is a monument to the Byzantines, of course, but, more recently a monument to the frankly troublesome idea that what was thought to be a great society and wonderful civilization in the Old South was built upon the historical fact that one race of people was held inferior to another. I suddenly felt that such a house built upon the grounds where the enslavement of others took place was not only a testament to the objective detachment achieved through scholarship but, ironically, evidence that as history repeats itself, the so-called paganisms often emerge to make their own contributions to that "wisdom" and that, indeed, we may all be enriched when that occurs.

Oddly, I thought then, this building suggests to me that a reorientation concerning knowledge may be possible; that out of Byzantium may come a real understanding of Justinian's *Digest of Laws*, allowing the human species to move forward from the medieval period toward true wisdom; that in the same way the world's inhabitants have made progress in the arts and sciences, in psychology and biology, the *laws of the indigenes* will move forward, and the great body of Indian law which began thousands of years ago with the Oral Traditions and has emerged into America in the twentieth century will bring knowledge and legislation which will not be seen in the future as barbaric, racist, or discriminatory. Yes, I thought, all things change. I went away encouraged as a writer, a teacher, a parent, though I never set foot in the Dumbarton Oaks library that day. Nor have I since.

Subsequently, I found out that Dumbarton Oaks has an annual budget of $6 million, much of it from its $20 million endowment, and a staff of sixty. I was filled with envy—and hope.

The condition of "library/book deprivation" still goes on in the places which are important to me. But this experience has suggested to me that for all of us who have come from places others consider nowhere to the modern academy, wishing to be scholars, there is the realization that when opposing cultural heritages, different aesthetic sensitivities, and different ways of looking at the world are cherished, all humanity can have hope for the future of its children.

12

America's Oldest Racism
The Roots of Inequality

In spite of many positive experiences in the academic world, America's oldest racism remains as troubling as ever.

A young East Indian-American scholar by the name of Dinesh D'Souza who is now a John M. Olin Scholar at the American Enterprise Institute in Washington, D.C., has called up the memory of an awful history by giving contemporary voice to the idea of "prudent/rational discrimination" as a virtuous practice for a democracy like America.[1] It is for some a good idea, the last word; for others, the new racism. For Indians the argument is an old idea that they know well, an idea which has been defended in America since the landing of Columbus.

Though I admit to being a little confused concerning D'Souza's particular stance on American Indians (they do not take a central position in any of his arguments), it is my understanding that he believes Europeans were quite justified in thinking themselves superior to Indians and implementing a firm policy to take over their lands. The right of one group to dominate another, he suggests, was not the result of biological racism but the result of "ethnocentric theories of cultural difference," and this reality, he says, makes the "progress" toward civilization which has characterized Western U.S. history a good and inevitable thing. His debatable point that the concept of race in the modern biological sense did not exist when the enslavement of Africans originally occurred in the fifteenth and sixteenth centuries has little connection to what happened to Indians during the nineteenth and twentieth centuries when two-thirds of their treaty-protected lands were stolen by America, nor does it connect with the continued colonial power exercised by the United States over Indian populations. Thus, if one looks at D'Souza's argument and the results of five hundred years of European occupation of native lands on this continent from the point of view of decimated native populations reduced to beggary in the country they occupied for thousands of years, the distinction hardly matters.

In suggesting that affirmative action as a national policy and civil rights activism as a social agenda are no longer necessary, D'Souza says that biological racism, which really raised its ugly head ideologically when Europeans first encountered non-Western peoples, is declining as a social force in America and that discrimination is a good thing if it is based on evidence rather than ideology. He wonders if we should define racism as a "doctrine of *intrinsic* superiority and inferiority" between groups. Before he convinces anyone of what that would mean in terms of actual behavior, he goes on to argue that, in the 1990s and beyond, there are circumstances in which discrimination, at least in the black/white context, makes sense and, furthermore, that prejudice may not be the result of ignorant predisposition (i.e., stereotype), as had once been thought; but rather, it may be one citizen's prudent judgment of another. It is a muddled argument, to be sure. Nevertheless, for the better part of the current decade, ever since D'Souza finished graduate studies at America's elitist institutions and began writing about "illiberal education," he has been touted by editors, scholars, and politicians alike as a new voice, a meritorious scholar of contemporary conservative thinking. The *Free Press* publishes his books; the *Atlantic Monthly* publishes his essays.

For the indigenous populations of this continent, from the Maya to the Cree, there is nothing new about D'Souza's thinking, nor does he bring substantive new evidence to his argument concerning the history and the consequences of racism in America. His argument is that affirmative action and the liberal civil rights programs have failed as social policy because their underlying ideas have not been based on the "reality of traits" attributed to specific racial groups. African Americans, he points out, do have a substantially higher crime rate than whites; therefore, for whites to fear them is not racist—just practical. Women do get pregnant and leave their jobs; therefore, it is sensible for employers to discriminate in favor of men in hiring practices. It is economically justified. He says that affirmative action treats competent individuals as incompetent and thus should be scrapped as social policy. He uses the prejudices of one group toward another to bolster his notion that it is not just whites who notice and discriminate. For example, he says that "49 percent of blacks and 68 percent of Asians say that Hispanics tend to have bigger families than they can support." This means, one supposes, that if Hispanics are poor, it is their own fault. He says virtually nothing about social policies toward indigenous populations which amount to colonial genocide, Termination/Relocation, jurisdiction, coercive assimilation, and so on.

One of the major flaws in almost all of D'Souza's discussion on race and equality in America is that it is based, as is all of the race discourse in this country since the Civil War, on the black/white paradigm almost exclusively. This exclusive and narrow look at American society has skewed the discourse on cause and effect to which we are all now subjected. D'Souza's contention is that the civil rights model as we know it, based as it is on prejudice and stereotype, would be denounced by Martin Luther King as wrong, even immoral. His interpretation of King's ideology on race, whether it is sensible or not, is convenient, because such a conclusion allows all of us to put aside the historical violence of the economic policies of a capitalistic democracy which are at the root of inequality in America. Such an argument is specious, also, because America's oldest racial act, the deliberate theft of a continent from its original inhabitants, could never have been accomplished without government intervention. If any acts in history have demonstrated the triumph of government regulation over the free market, the thefts of Indian lands do so. It was never a free market for the Sioux, who said to potential buyers, "The Black Hills are not for sale." They consented neither to the sale itself nor to the terms. Indeed, the federal government and the state governments have conspired in Indian land thefts for more than a hundred years. If the argument about race and equality in America is ever to be understood, the Indian experience in economics must become part of the discourse.

The rationale for America's oldest racism was never about slavery. It was never about the color of one's skin. The oldest racism in America was about the economically motivated, government-sponsored theft of lands occupied by others and the subsequent, deliberate murder of millions of Indians by the U.S. citizens and military. While one could argue that such activities would give support to D'Souza's call for the removal of government from the process, this has never been a reasoned interpretation of the American Indian experience, because the U. S. government has also represented a democratic "free market" based on the exploitation of resources for profit, an ideology which has always been anathema to native cultures on this continent.

The historical and deep-seated rationale for historical theft, dispossession, and inequality is exemplified by a Horatio Greenough sculpture called "Rescue Group," which was commissioned in 1837 and placed in the East Portico of the Capitol in Washington, D.C., some twenty years later. The sculpture has remained in the hearts and minds of Americans as an example of the intellectual ideals of a superior civilization. It shows the savage menacing white society, represented by a helpless woman and child, and a pioneer man towering over a dark Indian. According to D'Souza's thinking, this art could be said to be based on experience, not racial ideology. Indians did kill white pioneer families, so they deserved to be defeated and colonized. They did carry tomahawks in one hand and scalps in the other. This art, then, is not racist. It is very simply a logical image arising out of a realistic historical experience.

It is worth noting that at the same time Greenough was modeling his clay—indeed, as early as 1827—the Cherokee Nation, in an effort to save itself and its treaty-protected lands from American democracy, was adopting a constitution with the express purpose of establishing a national Cherokee government modeled upon American principles. It did them little good. Like the Jews who contributed to German culture for hundreds of years and then faced Hitler in the twentieth century, their efforts at participating as Indians in American culture in the middle of the nineteenth century were not only futile, they were considered absurd. The Georgia state legislature, while it did not send them to the ovens, wrote as follows:

Resolved, That all the lands appropriated and unappropriated within the conventional limits of Georgia, belong to her absolutely; that the title is in her; that the Indians are tenants at her will; that she may at any time she pleases determine their tenancy, by taking possession of the premises; and that Georgia has the right to extend her authority and laws over the whole territory, and to coerce obedience to them from all descriptions of people, be they white, red, or black, within her limits.

While many contemporary Americans believe the Jewish holocaust stands alone in the annals of racist crime, Indians who have survived in America are not so sure. D'Souza's argument seems to be trying to convince us that the action of the State of Georgia, which typifies hundreds of such actions across this land, was based on "rational discrimination"—that racism probably had little or nothing to do with it and was, in any case, efficacious. The Cherokees were "removed." The Supreme Court modified the "removal" and allowed the Cherokees to live subject to American law and power. America and the State of Georgia ascended, and the Cherokee Nation today like all of the Indian nations of this land, considers itself among the bare survivors of racist America. Contrarily, D'Souza might suggest that to absorb and assimilate the unwilling Cherokees for the purpose of colonization was only "Amer-centric," not racist. Thus, to confer American citizenship (in 1924) upon a population that neither wanted it nor requested it, can't be considered anti-Indian or racist, since their"agreement" was documented. The people of the white power structures of America who managed social policy during this removal era were as driven by the ideals of market capitalism as are D'Souza's colleagues today. To steal Indian lands for profit then was simply an economic issue, and today it continues to be a matter of good economics to defend these policies and, in the process, transcend ethnic cultures.

The argument in defense of this kind of Indian history is the same defense D'Souza advocates for the continued well-being of America. It is not racism to discriminate, his argument says, because "people's perceptions of others are always filtered through the lens of their own prior experiences," the "distilled product of many years of experience." Moreover, these acts are efficient; they make economic and common sense.

If you agree that such discrimination "forces a choice in which the claims of morality are on one side, and the claims of rationality and productivity are on the other," so be it, says D'Souza's argument. The choices he gives simply leaves out Indians who even today, through some miracle or unaccountable oversight, continue to possess thousands of acres of land and historical rights as citizens of Indian nations. He puts everything into a civil rights mode, ignoring the treaty rights model which is the true basis for American Indian history. For Americans of the future, D'Souza suggests, the choices are threefold: first, racial preference could be treated as an essential remedy (one wonders if this could mean the defense of native nationhood); second, all discrimination, including rational discrimination, could be considered illegal in both the public and private sectors (one wonders if this means the federal government and state governments would be forced to stop colonial practices on Indian lands); or, third—clearly D'Souza's preference—rational discrimination could be made legal and civil rights legislation be repudiated. What would become of two hundred years of agonized defense of Indian rights, property, and sovereignty under the contrived paradigm of these three choices is left to the imagination.

The modern dialogue and the history of Indians on this continent leads one to cynicism about the possibility that the average American and the average Indian can define the world in terms of mutually acceptable ideals. Because the debate on race and society in America, at least since the Civil War, has been almost entirely about black and white, the end of slavery, and the new immigrants and diversity, the hope of the American public was for a time that desegregation would bring the end of racism. Some say the end of racism as a widespread phenomenon has, indeed, come to pass. Though others say the hopes for solutions to racial conflict under present circumstances are getting more and more difficult, optimists like D'Souza believe that harmony is possible and that there is no longer any need for public policy in desegregating blacks and whites, nor any federal intervention of any kind. People today are in regular contact with each other, these optimists say, and they no longer have false views of one another; their newly formulated, clear images of one another promote racial harmony, and *continued assimilation will make oppression of one group by another group impossible.*

Such idealization of a long and troubled racial history has made any modern civil rights debate almost meaningless to the Native Americans who are citizens of Indian nations in this country. Because these debates are based on the experiences of blacks, whites, and new immigrants, the result has been a failure to understand that for equality and democracy to be defined according to the original constitutional and aboriginal intent, Indians must be seen as Indians, not as ethnic individuals in America. They must be seen as the original peoples, possessing dual citizenship in their own tribal nation(s) as well as in the United States. They must be seen as nations of people who occupied this continent for thousands of years with personal and national rights and who still do.

The problem with much of what D'Souza writes is not that it is ahistorical; rather, it is a return to a failed history of justice for America's first peoples. Of course, D'Souza readily admits that he is not a historian of either society or ideas. His point is that affirmative action as public policy and the repeal of the Civil Rights Act of 1964 are necessary if the black/white dialogue is to improve and if blacks are ever to achieve parity. Indians are not in this discourse, nor have they ever been his concern.

His argument, however, for the return of individual rights unfettered by government and his enthusiastic defense of the traditions of the West and of progress toward civilization are frightening. They deny again the right of Native America to see its Indianness as separate from mainstream Americanism, and they put at risk much of the work done by native scholars in academia over the past thirty years in the development of Native American Studies as a defensive mechanism for unique tribal experience and knowledge. It excludes participation by Indians as anything but "ethnic minorities."

For Indian country today, D'Souza's argument seems to defend colonization by economics and conquest by assimilation. What's new about that?

13

End of the Failed Metaphor

It is hard to say what will survive and why as the world moves forward. Only in retrospect can that be known. As I think about the writing we are doing currently as Native Americans, I am disappointed in the congeniality of most of it, because in the face of astonishing racism of one people toward another, there continues to be great risk. My thoughts turn with some trepidation to survival and place, the New World, and the old—this place once known only by the tribes but a place at once named, described, misnamed, and renamed by those who followed the colonist's prince.

My thoughts are about the nature of our lives as indigenous peoples in the modern world, and the nature of our survival, and because I am a writer, the function of literary voice. In the twentieth century, the survival of indigenous peoples everywhere, not just here in my homelands, but everywhere in the world, has been nothing if not miraculous. In the face of efficient colonial land theft, which has made us poor, the environmental wastelands caused by virulent economic interests, the attempted ethnocide, deicide, and genocide brought about by the failure of one federal policy after another toward our peoples, we continue to say, *anpetu wi*, the sun, lives on forever. And we continue to say that we will forever call him *tunkashina*, "Grandfather." *Tunkashinayapi*—"All of our grandfathers surround us." This continuation is, truly, a miracle. *Anpetu wi*, the day light, to whom we speak in our prayers, is symbolic of the cultural spirit of the Sioux in traditional terms. Every day, every glimpse of the sun reminds us of who we are and to whom we are related.

What I want to focus on in this last essay of this collection has to do with the emblematic use of our histories and cultures outside of those traditions to tell our stories. I want to focus on the literary creations, that is, the symbols and metaphors which are developed in contemporary literary terms and in foreign places outside of our traditional languages and lifeways to describe who we are and where we have been. This seems appropriate in this last decade of the century, during which we have paid much attention to the quincentennial of "discovery."

Indigenous peoples are no longer in charge of what is imagined about them, and this means that they can no longer freely imagine themselves as they once were and as they might become. Perhaps a separation of culture and place and voice has never been more contextualized in modernity than it is for Indians today. This means that the literary metaphors devised for the purposes of illumination belong more often than not to those outside of the traditional spheres. What comes immediately to mind is the metaphor of Mother Earth, and others such as the characterization of the literary figure, the Trickster.

Mother Earth, some have argued, was really an example of the evolution of female earth imagery in Europe rather than in North America; therefore, she rightly becomes available to every writer in all of Christendom. She is used to express a wide variety of ideals and has accounted for a number of arguments between scholars. In this essay I review some personal issues concerning the use of metaphor and pose some questions which may be useful in analyzing the consequences of literary acts.

As spring came upon us a few years ago, I was asked to participate in the Great Plains Writer's Conference at South Dakota State University, my alma mater. This was to be the first time I had returned to that place since the late 1950s, and I was overcome by nostalgia. It was there, in the college town of Brookings in central South Dakota, miles away from my home reservation, that I first met a tall, young Minneconjou Sioux from Cheyenne River, just back from Korea. My father, a Santee, had known of this young man's French and Indian family for generations, so our meeting seemed somehow fortuitous; we married and had children together. And then we left one another—and that was the end of that story. Such a return to what might be called a place of origin, however, as this recent visit to my old alma mater reminded me of what Sarte was supposed to have said, that the greatest happiness is always a little sad, and so I walked about the streets alone during the first few hours, recalling the events of a past life.

At the conference table the next morning, we were asked to move out of our own individual spheres and speculate about broader historical matters. The year was 1990, one hundred years after the Wounded Knee massacre, and our conference title was "Wounded Knee: The Literary Legacy." We were there to speculate specifically about "Wounded Knee as Metaphor for Tragedy." I read a poem about Wounded Knee which

I had written years earlier. The first line was, "All things considered, Crow Dog should be removed." The second line was, "With Sitting Bull dead, it was easier said." I thought about Shelley, the great English poet who told the literati of his day that poetry was supposed to be a mirror which makes beautiful that which is distorted. That kind of theory seemed indefensible at that conference. The bleak truth is that even my subversive sensibility concerning poetry was invaded that day, and I left as soon as the conference ended.

From there I went to the University of South Dakota, another college campus a couple of hours' drive away at Vermillion, South Dakota, where I participated in a discussion entitled "Land, Law, and Ethics," with many white and Indian scholars, politicians, and tribal leaders who are locked into a pathology of racial hatred and good intentions as complex as any in the world, in a state where the largest daily newspaper refuses to call the killing of innocent women and children at Wounded Knee, all of them under a white flag of truce, a "massacre." In South Dakota it is publicly called, one hundred years after the fact, an "event," "an incident," or an "affair." And now, poets were invited to speak on the idea of Wounded Knee as a metaphor for tragedy.

These two incidents are responsible, more than any others in recent times, for my renewed interest in and present discussion of the function of literary device. Out of these experiences, I have formed questions to which I have no answers. What are the consequences of such metaphors? What is the effect of taking one of the most vicious criminal acts in history and imagining it as literary device? What happens to history? What happens morally and ethically to the people in such a process? Will our children know who their relatives are? Will they be able to know themselves in the context of a new history, a literary history rather than an actual one? Is it possible that poetry flattens value systems, so that what was once not talked about becomes useful only for sensation?

When I returned to my office at Eastern Washington University after these public events, I read quite by accident "The New World Man," an essay by the gifted, Spanish-speaking novelist Rudolfo Anaya. It is an essay in which he analyzes the important metaphor with which this essay began, the metaphor of Mother Earth.

Anaya says that the people in the Southwest are the "fruit of the Spanish Father and the Indian Mother." He alternately labels them Hispanic and Chicano. He glorifies Malinche, who was the first Indian woman of Mexico to bear children fathered by a Spaniard. Without talking much about the fact that she was a captive of men and had little free choice in the matter of who was to father her children, Anaya says "in our mothers is embodied the archetype of the indigenous Indian Mother of the Americas," and he urges that "it is her nature we must know." As I read this essay I wondered how I could understand this glorification within the context of Wounded Knee.

I recognized Anaya's glorification as similar to the argument for the glorification of Sacajawea, the Plains Indian girl (barely in her teens, we are told) who led Lewis and Clark, the precursors of those who stole the land and forced millions into Christianity against their wills, the Shoshone youngster who eventually lived with the Frenchman Charbonneau and died bearing his children. Pocohantas and Tekakwitha also came to mind. And I began to understand that, as American Indian literatures are often used to serve the white man's needs, so the Indian woman archetype is used for the colonist's pleasure and profit.

We have all become collaborators without intention, and we all bear responsibility for our common histories. It is not just those people (the colonists) who came and invaded the lives and lands of our ancestors, implanted their seed and began from that moment on to contend their ownership. It is what we have done to ourselves. Thinking of collaborators, I flipped the pages of an unpublished manuscript lying on my desk and read a poem I had written years before, in 1980, that expressed the troubling fracture in which I saw us living our lives:

Collaborator
Ensuring Domestic Tranquility

I remember the fallen trees, thin and pale as frost smoke;
and how the wounded river's rippling presence,
witness to the outrage, intentionally or not,
consoled the venal among us. Poor, wind-swept,
the miles and miles of prairie dog towns
kept our secret. We swam and knew this could become the
    place
of the unburied, here where the peace treaty
was signed and it was said crimes on both sides
would be forgotten. Buzzards and Old Spotted Eagle
kept watch.

In this mythological Hades descendants
of cowpokes, stirring the tainted water with glimmerous
wands meant to disrupt the questions we would ask
about the sweet creation of life, and death,
and meaning, take up residence in Buffalo Gap,

the farthest fields. Jedediah Smith was said to tear the hide
from grizzlies, his life inimical to the lives of all living things.
Thin, pale children run
on Cedar street.

Persistent jets, unseen and ominous
as the shrill of the imagined Red Telephone
whisper in the river's gorge, lapping at the water's edge.
And I walk, intentional or not, amongst
the tourists who are here again
to see the Indians dance.

Forgive me, my children.
I barely hear the soft raindrops on shrouded drums
of my father and his father. And yours.

Periodic, unpredictable,
their songs sway in the gloom
of my forfeiture.

This poem suggests that we all bear the weight of history. It suggests
that poets must ask, what is our responsibility, and what of the future?
Anaya poses the question in his essay very specifically, I think, but we
may generalize it for the purposes of this discussion. Anaya says, "As I
think of the quincentennial of Columbus's crossing, I ask myself how I
relate to that Hispanic legacy which left the peninsula in 1492 to implant
itself in the New World. How do I relate to the peninsular consciousness
of the people who crossed the Atlantic five hundred years ago to deposit
their seed on the earth of the New World?"

This is the essential question for all of us who are now called Native
American writers, or Third World writers, to answer. It is especially
important for those of us who are native women writers. For myself, I
am reluctant to forget about *anpetu wi* (just as I am reluctant to talk of
Wounded Knee in terms of metaphor), for I know that without *anpetu
wi*, the *indigenous* male presence, Mother Earth is a silent, barren place
of death.

I shudder at Anaya's answer, which rings with confidence and finality: "I am the son of Spanish and Mexican colonists who settled the
fertile Rio Grand Valley of New Mexico. I am the New World Man I have
sought: I am an indigenous man taking his essence and perspective from
the earth and people of the New World, from the Earth which is my
Mother. By naming ourselves Chicanos we reaffirmed our humanity by

exploring and understanding the nature of our mothers, the indigenous American woman."

He describes his duality in this way: "The Spanish character is the aggressive, conquest-oriented part of our identity; the Native American nature is the more harmonious, earth-oriented side." He calls for the assimilation of those two natures.

The fragility of this resolution lies in Anaya's willful dismissal of indigenous myth. Yet he must know that there are no versions of origin, no discussions of wisdom, goodness, kindness, hospitality, nor any of the other virtues of indigenous, tribal society without the seed, and spirit, and power of the indigenous fathers. There is no mythic cycle from the spiritual journey into the real world that is not associated with both indigenous maleness and femaleness. What about the lands the people say they possess, lands which are possessed legitimately both in the recent treaty process and in the ancient imagination?

I want to ask about the utter disregard of this maleness as it is dismissed by the colonists of the past and the present in favor of the mother goddess as lone repositor of history. For those who have prayed to *tunkashinayapi*, there is the certain knowledge that the earth's survival is not possible without those indigenous male figures, those rights of possession, that occupancy, that vision.

To accept the indigenous woman's role as the willing and cooperating recipient of the colonist's seed and as the lone repositor of culture is to legitimize the destruction of ancient religions, the murder of entire peoples, the rape of the land, not to mention the out-and-out theft of vast native homelands. To do so dismisses the centuries of our modern American Indian histories when our fathers fought and died and made treaties in order to save us from total annihilation.

Metaphor has sometimes been used, if not to legitimize colonization, then to tolerate it in the modern world. "Wounded Knee as Metaphor for Tragedy" implies the absence of human control in the killing of hundreds of Indians. Nothing could be more wrong, and conferring medals of heroism on the killer troops exposes the lie of it. Because America refuses to reject its colonial past, it continues its acts of destruction, murder, rape, and theft. We will read, therefore, in our morning newspapers that a waste dump is to be put on top of the traditional burial mounds of the Yakima Indian people of Washington State; that the U.S. courts have ruled, again, against the indigenous religious leaders of the peyote religion, as old as any in the world, and harassment of its communicants will continue. We will hear that some members of the Senate Select Committee on Indian Affairs have vowed secretly that they will never allow hearings on the legislative proposal for the return of stolen land in the sacred Black Hills to its rightful owners. We will watch while white affluent Americans tie green paper ribbons on trees on Earth Day (more metaphors) and drive away from the scene in the latest, gas-guzzling automobiles, the most potent producers of the toxic gases which cause global warming.

In order for these crimes to be stopped, they must be recognized as emblematic of the dismissal of our native fathers in favor of our colonial ones. In the final analysis, you see, what kind of seed is implanted matters to Mother Earth. To continue to use her as a receptacle for the seeds of exploitation and extermination against her will holds no promise for the future.

The function of metaphor is to clarify, to illuminate, not to add to the confusion. Many other writers of America have taken up the issues of a ruined world. Many have contemplated the meaning of the mother goddesses of all times, though they seldom spend much time asking why or how we reached Gilead, only saying that we are there. America's colonial past, its dismissal of indigenous maleness, its glorification of the fecund native woman as bearer of alien children, the continuing aggressiveness of the colonist 's exploitation of the earth for profit may be the essential causes of the horrors of Gilead. Margaret Atwood does not tell us that in her horrific *Handmaid's Tale*. But, she certainly illustrates what happens when we fail to know the function of history and metaphor.

And so, as I raise more questions than I can answer, I want to say that we must resist the argument that the American Mother Earth, the native earth, should be legitimized as receptacle for the male colonist's seed, for it leads to a new and disastrous religion in which *anpetu wi* and *tunkashina* cannot collaborate. I would like to suggest, also, that there are at least two unexamined moral axioms in this argument that have kept the audience we have clamoring to hear more of the theory of the female-indigenous receptacle of the colonist's seed. The first is that there is no male seed which is indigenous; it has, as expected, vanished. The second is that even if there were such a survivor, he is not deserving, and he must not, therefore, be allowed to compete for his own life either historically or imaginatively.

To what extent our recent Native American literatures have expressed, denied, or trivialized our reality depends, one supposes, on the ways of thinking which have captured the public's attention. For now, we contend with the idea that Crazy Horse is either an alcoholic drink or a steak house in California, that Dakota is a pick-up with four-wheel drive, and the Braves are alive and well in Atlanta doing the toma-hawk chop.

Metaphors are complex and disturbing things. We must claim them when they are useful to our literary legacies and disclaim them when they are failed. If we do not, we will have become the hired intellectuals of the disciplines of academia that we have so often feared. For the Sioux Oyate, the male creator figures are inseparable from the female. They are inseparable from specific geography. They have been with us in life and death and at Wounded Knee. How dare we suggest that Mahpiyato, Inyan, Tunkashina, Anpetu Wi and all the other fathers of the people are nonexistent, irrelevant, undeserving, and thus appropriately displaced by the colonist's seed in our Mother. How dare we say that crimes of history are mere tragedy for which no one but God is responsible?

We must make hard choices if we expect the plot to keep moving.

Notes

Selected Bibliography

Notes

Chapter 2. *The Broken Cord*

1. There was a film made of this story, and it ran on commercial television a few months after the tragic accidental death of Adam.

Chapter 5. Why I Can't Read Wallace Stegner

1. Many of the references in this essay can be found in Wallace Stegner, *Wolf Willow* (Penguin Books, 1961), and in *Conversations with Wallace Stegner on Western History and Literature*, a collaboration between Wallace Stegner and Richard W. Etulain with a forward by Norman Cousins (University of Utah Press, 1983).

2. Peter Matthiessen's *In the Spirit of Crazy Horse* (Viking Press, 1983) became a notable piece of investigative writing based on material obtained through the Freedom of Information Act. Matthiessen argued that Leonard Peltier, now in prison for killing two FBI agents during the Wounded Knee 1973 "takeover" by the American Indian Movement, did not get a fair trial. The book enraged many anti-Indian forces in South Dakota and was forced off the bookshelves for a brief period through litigation by William Janklow, a former governor who in 1994, after several years absence, was reelected to an unprecedented fourth term. Matthiessen wrote that Janklow had raped a young Sioux woman when he was working on the reservation in the Legal Services program. In 1967 Janklow was quoted as saying, "The only way to deal with the Indian problem in South Dakota is to put a gun to the AIM leaders' heads and pull the trigger." He gave voice to the sentiment of a large portion of the South Dakota public.

Chapter 6. A Centennial Minute from Indian Country

1. I have many books on my shelves with titles like *What Great Philosophers Thought about God*, and *The Great Republic and Master Historians*. The *Life and Labors of Bishop Hare, Apostle to the Sioux*, by M. A. DeWolfe Howe (Sturgis and Walton, 1911) has been in my library for years. I don't know how I came to possess it. Perhaps my parents had it, for they, too, were collectors of old books

153

and critics of hegemony no matter what its origin. This essay started out as a simple commentary on the centennial because I was asked to give talks at various places. Then it turned into a book review of that old 1911 book and, finally, a critique of the church and colonialism.

Chapter 7. The Relationship of a Writer to the Past

1. The Sioux claim that the Black Hills were taken illegally is, of course, one of the major stories of the Sioux. It permeates all contemporary discourse. For those curious about how long it takes Indian tribes to pursue land claims, take a look at this documentation of litigation. In 1920 the Sioux claim was filed in the Court of Claims. Various courts acted on this claim in 1942, 1943, 1946, 1950, 1954, 1958, 1961, 1968, 1974, 1975, 1978, 1979, 1980, 1981, 1982, and 1985. (See the *Wicazo Sa Review* 4, no. 1 [Spring, 1988]: 43). In 1980, the Supreme Court wrote a decision on this matter, saying it was a "rank and ripe" case of theft, and authorized a money settlement. For over a decade, the people of the Sioux Nation have refused to accept payment, calling instead for a political solution and the return of lands.

2. The Sinte Gleska College Lakota Studies Department, Victor Douville, Chairman, "Hanto Yo: Authentic Farce, A Critical Review" (Mission, South Dakota: 1980).

3. In a brief discussion of Wole Soyinka, John Updike sees the African writer as "a formidable egghead," calling him "an analyst first, a propagandist second." This is, one supposes, a compliment, yet there is the notion that critics of color and culture when they enter into the discussion of race are preaching some kind of gospel, not analyzing facts of history. It is interesting that Updike, himself a white, male member of a prosperous and efficient Euro-American (i.e., white) capitalist democracy has not been called, to my knowledge, a propagandist (nor have his colleagues). See Updike's *Hugging the Shore* (Ecco, 1983).

4. The issues of identity and authenticity are a major concern to Indian scholars and to the Sioux in particular. Nontribal writers over the years have created historical tableaux using "informants," and as a result a special kind of history has developed which might be called "the disruption of traditional history." An examination of that disruption has already begun, and I predict that this will be a major subject of research in the twenty-first century.

5. Buffalohead's essay appeared on pp. 156–57 of *Indian Self-Rule*, edited by Kenneth R. Philp (Salt Lake City: Howe Brothers, 1986).

6. A rejoinder appeared in the *American Studies Journal* in September, 1993, written by Dr. Arnold Krupat, a professor and critic from Sarah Lawrence College in New York. He makes several points, including the following: that literatures of resistance must be literatures of comparativism in this era of "multiculturalism"; that native scholars are as capable of poor reasoning as anyone else; that the "parameters" of Native Studies cannot be defended because

they shift; that Indians are simply doing intellectual police work, and they do it in a dismissive, contemptuous tone; that such work which is essentially anti-intellectual and counterproductive and will eventually play into the hands of cultural conservatives, and Indian scholars will become intellectually disreputable; that literatures cannot "belong" to a people; and that to be born an Indian is not enough. The identity issue is largely dismissed by Krupat, since it is his view that Indian scholars are not "determiners" of Indian cultures due to their training by the academies and the support of grants. Finally, he says that there is no "sovereignty" in an absolute sense, and the Indian scholar's arguments for that claim are largely "polemical."

Chapter 8. The American Indian Fiction Writers

1. Books referred to in this essay are as follows: José David Saldívar, *The Dialectics of Our America: Geneology, Cultural Critique, and Literary History* (Duke University Press, 1991); Wole Soyinka, *Art, Dialogue, and Outrage* (Pantheon, 1988–1993); Edward W. Said, *The Politics of Dispossession* (Pantheon, 1994), and *Culture and Imperialism* (Knopf, 1993); Cornel West, *Race Matters* (Beacon Press, 1993); Dominick Lacapra, *The Bounds of Race: Perspectives on Hegemony and Resistance* (Cornell University, 1991); Timothy Brennan, *Salman Rushdie and the Third World: Myths of Nation* (St. Martin's Press, 1989); Homi K. Bhabha, *Nation and Narration* (Routledge, 1990); Lennard J. Davis and M. Bella Mirabella, eds., *Left Politics and the Literary Profession* (Columbia University Press, 1990); Frank Chin, ed., *The Big AIIIEEEEE* (Meridian, 1991).

Chapter 9. The American Indian Woman in the Ivory Tower

1. I refer to an old Dakota myth of origin in this prose poem. I really don't know if this has been written down or recorded anywhere, since it was told to me by this grandmother, and I assume it to be one of those stories that tells of that period when the Dakotahs were becoming the Star People. I know this story only in Dakota language and have not heard it in English. Life originates in water, in this telling, and the *unktechies* were there, and it is said they observed a rainbow. The creator flung a rib into the water and brought about a female, and they were to find the earth. They would be helped in this task by two birds and two animals. (When I have talked with others about this and asked about who the helpers were and how they could be described in English, I was told they were the loon, the gull, the beaver, and the muskrat.) The loon begins the search by diving, and the muskrat ends it by swimming very far and powerfully from the east toward the west, scouting. There are many versions of this story and, of course, it is a long story, much longer than this reference would suggest. It is a story which belongs to the people and, I think, the Sissetons in particular; therefore, perhaps it is to remain in the oral tradition. My

grandmother always ended her telling of this with a song, since, she said, the *unktechies* gave the people their medicine songs at that time. I do not personally remember the songs, though I know there are singers in South Dakota who do know them.

2. The movie *A River Runs Through It* was based on a book written by Norman Maclean and published in 1976 by the University of Chicago Press. It was Maclean's first book (he was a professor at the University of Chicago) and the first book of fiction published by that press. The movie and the new edition available from Pocket Books in New York, were popularized in 1992.

Chapter 10. The Big Pipe Case

1. This piece, subtitled "Criminalization of Alcoholism: A Native Feminist View" first appeared as a newspaper series in *Indian Country Today*, Rapid City, South Dakota, as a four-part series in 1993. Dianne Zephier-Bird, a young Sioux attorney, collaborated on this writing, and the events described are on public record. Some names have been changed to respect privacy.

2. I first heard about this case from a relative and talked to many people before I wrote this article. I wish to publicly thank my friend and collaborator, Diane Zephier, who helped me work out the legal issues in this story. The fictitious name of Big Pipe comes from the fictive world described in some of my stories (*The Power of Horses*) and in my novel (*From the River's Edge*) published in the early 1990s by Arcade, Little/Brown. In actuality, the teenaged victim in this story comes from a very well-known and important family on the Crow Creek and Lower Brule Reservations in South Dakota. What this has meant to us as a tribal people is that if it could happen to her, it could happen to any one of us or our daughters. The Indian Child Welfare Act was passed November 8, 1978.

Chapter 12. America's Oldest Racism

1. D'Souza's essay, "America's Oldest Racism," refers to another of his works, *The End of Racism* (Free Press, 1995). It refers also to various newspaper reviews, including "Demonizing the American Dilemma" (*New York Review of Books*, October 19, 1995, p. 10), by George Fredrickson.

Selected Bibliography

Part 1

Dorris, Michael. *The Broken Cord*. New York and Los Angeles: Harper & Row, 1989.

Clifton, James. A., ed. *The Invented Indian: Cultural Fictions and Government Policies*. New Brunswick, NJ: Transaction Publishers, 1990.

Deloria, Vine, Jr. *Custer Died for Your Sins*. New York: Macmillian, 1969.

Deloria, Vine, Jr. *We Talk, You Listen*. New York: Macmillian, 1970.

Deloria, Vine, Jr. "Comfortable Fictions and the Struggle for Turf: An Essay Review of *The Invented Indian*." *American Indian Quarterly* 16 (Summer, 1992).

Guthrie, Patricia. "Alcohol's Child: A Father Tells His Tale." *New York Times Book Review*. 1989.

Haynes, Johnson. *Sleepwalking through History: America through the Reagan Years*. New York: W. W. Norton, 1991.

Lazarus, Edward. *Black Hills, White Justice*. New York and Los Angeles: Harper-Collins, 1991.

McLaughlin's Annual Report, August 26, 1891. Annual Report. 1891, p. 334. *My Friend The Indian*. Lincoln: University of Nebraska Press, 1989 (reprint).

Niehardt, John. *Black Elk Speaks*. Lincoln and London: University of Nebraska Press, 1932.

O'Neil, Floyd A., June K. Lyman, and Susan McKay, eds. *Wounded Knee, 1973*. Lincoln and London: University of Nebraska Press, 1984.

Young Bear, Ray. *Black Eagle Child: The Facepaint Narratives*. Ames: University of Iowa Press, 1992.

Part 2

American Association of Colleges for Teacher Education in collaboration with Teacher Corps. U. S. Office of Education, Washington, DC, August, 1978.

Berkhofer, Robert F. *The White Man's Indian: Images of the American Indian from Columbus to the Present*. New York: Knopf, 1978; New York; Vintage Books, 1879.

Matthiessen, Peter. *In the Spirit of Crazy Horse*. New York: Viking, 1980.

Stegner, Wallace. *Wolf Willow*. New York: Viking, 1963.

Part 3

Brennan, Timothy. *Salman Rushdie and the Third World: Myths of Nation*. New York: St. Martin's Press, 1989.

Buffalohead, Roger. "Self-Rule in the Past and the Future: An Overview." In Philip S. Deloria, ed. *Indian Self-Rule: First Hand Accounts of Indian-White Relations from Roosevelt to Reagan*. Salt Lake City: Utah Press, 1986.

Coltelli, Laura. ed. *Winged Words: American Indian Writers Speak*. American Indian Lives. Lincoln: University of Nebraska Press, 1990.

Douville, Victor. "Hanta Yo: Authentic Farce, a Critical Review." The Sinte Gleska College Lakota Studies Department, Rosebud, South Dakota. Feb. 8, 1980. Available from SGC archives.

Hill, Ruth Beebe. *Hanta Yo*. New York: Doubleday, 1979.

Said, Edward W. *Culture and Imperialism*. New York: Knopf, 1993.

Soyinka, Wole. *Myth, Literature, and the African World*. Cambridge: Cambridge University Press, 1976.

Part 4

Brownmiller, Susan. *Against Our Will: Men, Women and Rape*. New York: Simon & Schuster, 1975.